HOW TO BECOME A CELEBRITY

BUILDING A CAREER IN THE LIMELIGHT

CHARLES HOPKINS-THYME

Monaco 2013

©**ACANEXUS**, Monaco 2013

ISBN 978-82-92944-06-6

All rights reserved. No part of this publication may be reproduced, stored in a retrieval system, or transmitted in any form, or by any means, electronic, mechanical, recording, photocopying, or otherwise without the express written permission of the author.

Warning: The doing of an unauthorized act in relation to copyright work may result in both a civil claim for damages and criminal prosecution.

Although the author has tried to make the information as accurate as possible at the time of writing, no responsibility for any loss, injury, or inconvenience sustained by anyone using the information can be accepted. The mentioning of companies, individuals, or services in this book does not represent an endorsement; all normal due diligence should be carried out before entering into any contract.

First Edition: March 2013
Author: Charles Hopkins-Thyme
Production: Acanexus Publishing Ltd
Cover design and layout: Jana Rade, impact studios

CONTENTS

1. Celebrities – modern royalty 7
2. Find your real talents 13
3. Study hard 21
4. Persistence 31
5. Building an image 37
6. Get noticed 51
7. Become a seller 61
8. Working with agents 101
9. Things to remember 115
10. Appendix 119
    Actors' and performers' unions 119
    Talent agents 131
    Acting and voice coaches 147
    General web resources for actors and performers . . 165

Index 179

1 CELEBRITIES — MODERN ROYALTY

This is a practical book. It is intended to show you in a practical and feasible way how you can gain celebrity status—and reap the benefits that go with it. For that reason I'm not going into long theoretical discussions or reciting page after page of historical facts. But I do want to start with a brief outline of the history of the word "celebrity." The reason for doing so will soon become clear. The word first appeared, in its modern meaning, in The Oxford English Dictionary in 1849. But it really entered everyday language only when an explosive growth of the popular press and mass literacy made it possible for a person's reputation to be spread swiftly and widely across social and physical borders. And the power and importance of celebrities have continued to grow along with our means of communication and the mass media.

> "Celebrity" first appeared in The Oxford English Dictionary in 1849

> The importance of celebrities has continued to grow with the introduction of mass media

The considerable social and structural changes during the late 19th century and early 20th are considered other important factors in explaining the modern fascination with celebrities. Urbanization and the

> Urbanization and breakup of the extended family

8 | **How to Become a Celebrity**

mobility of individuals led to a breakup of the extended family and less close contact between people in local communities. Many researchers believe that reading about the life of celebrities fills a void left by the loss of close personal contact—and that knowing details about celebrities' day-to-day lives not only substitutes for local gossip but also gives the reader a feeling of belonging.

> Less close contact between people in local communities

> Celebrity gossip gives the reader a feeling of belonging

Let's not forget either that modern life can be—let's be honest here—damn boring. And reading about people with exciting lifestyles helps lift the monotony.

> Celebrities help lift the monotony of life

So, that's the history lesson done for the entire book. Why did I bother to tell you all this when you really just want to know what to do to get an agent, land a big gig, and wake up famous tomorrow? Because understanding the reason for why people need celebrities is essential in order to give people what they want. Why do so few celebrities live nice, quiet lives? Why do so many celebrities apparently have a scandalous side? Because celebrities who don't, aren't celebrities. They are just "good actors" or "great singers." Being just good, or even famous, doesn't make you a celebrity. Anyone can be famous. Parachute naked from the Empire State Building with a cat on your head and you will be famous. But

> Understanding people's need for celebrities is vital to achieve success

> Celebrity scandals

> Celebrities are not just "famous"

1: Celebrities – Modern Royalty

being famous in that way doesn't really fill the void that people are looking to true celebrities to fill. Sure, the media will write a few pages about you, and you'll get your 15 minutes of fame, but it won't make you a celebrity. People simply won't identify with you; they don't want to gossip about you and they don't want to live your life.

If you want to be a celebrity—a real celebrity, not just a well-known person—you need to make sure you fill those voids that the modern life has left. You must cater to the news hungry media, but you must also be likable enough for people to feel a relationship with you; you must give people something to talk about and your life must be interesting enough to offer something exciting to people whose lives are just plain boring. Keep that in mind when reading the rest of this book and when planning your career.

Fill the voids that modern life has left

Cater to news hungry media

Now, you may ask yourself why you would want to be a celebrity in the first place. Isn't it enough just to be really good at your profession, be it acting, singing or modeling—whatever profession you are looking to break into?

Why should you want to be a celebrity?

Being a celebrity certainly has its downside. Your life suddenly becomes very complicated. First of all, you give away your privacy

Downsides of being a celebrity

completely. Look at the points above and you will realize that you cannot be a celebrity—and cater to the people's need for news and gossip—and at the same time keep your private life private. No one wants to read about how well you have been doing at work or where you traveled on business last week. They want to feel they know you personally; they want to gossip about you. "Did you *see* how quickly she learned her lines for that new play?" simply doesn't cut it. You must be prepared to trade away your privacy if you want celebrity status.

<small>Loss of private life</small>

Then, of course, you have a whole range of other problems that come with a celebrity status. Stalkers obviously are irritating and sometimes a very serious security concern. The paparazzi will make sure you can hardly go out of our front door, so be prepared to wave goodbye to most "normal" activities like shopping at a local supermarket or eating at your local burger restaurant. If the paparazzi are not enough to make you go mad, then the constant attention from anyone around you—filming you with mobile cameras or asking for an autograph—is sure to keep you away from most public places.

<small>Stalkers and paparazzi</small>

You may also quickly find that you suddenly get a lot of new friends, which is nice until you

<small>Who are your real friends?</small>

1: Celebrities – Modern Royalty

start asking yourself where these people were three years ago when you were broke and struggling. Or even worse, where will they be three years from now when you have a brief problem with your career? Knowing if you can trust a friend or not is a constant worry of a celebrity. Will your friends suddenly sell the photos they took at a compromising moment—or will they deceive you and try to take your money? Then you have the constant—and I mean absolutely constant—negative comments about you in the media, on blogs, on Facebook, on Twitter. It suddenly seems that no matter what you do, someone will say or write something negative about you. They will criticize your looks, your clothes, your lifestyle, your latest performance. Whenever you open a magazine or Google your own name you will find enough crap about you to make even the most self-confident go insane. Ask any celebrity, and he or she will tell you that for the first few years in the spotlight they were just flabbergasted by "facts" reported about themselves in the media. To top it all off, you have to deal with the constant concern that it may all be taken away at any time. The media made you—and they can just as easily break you. The list is long of has-been stars whose names and photos appear only in the back pages of gossip magazines with headlines only to underline how far they have fallen since their heydays—and that is not a good list to be on.

	Trust issues
	Negative media focus
	The media are not concerned about the truth

How to Become a Celebrity

Celebrity status gives advantages that money can't buy

So why do it? Why try to achieve this celebrity status when there are plenty of successful people whom you hardly ever hear of. I mean, how many people on the Forbes list of the richest people in America would you actually recognize on the street?

With celebrity status come money-making opportunities

The fact is that you don't need celebrity status to become rich or successful. But it makes it a hell of a lot easier. Numerous celebrities have become budding business moguls and established themselves as very successful entrepreneurs. Their names have become brands worth millions of dollars. And the celebrity status, despite its many downsides, offers something that money really can't buy. It gives you a status and importance in society that can only be rivaled by perhaps the top of our political leadership. More people will listen to what a celebrity has to say on a subject he or she may know nothing about than to a senator who has served his state all his professional life. Celebrities are the new royalty. So is it worth all the hassle and stress and hard work? Of course it is!

Celebrities are the new royalty

2 FIND YOUR REAL TALENTS

If you want to become a celebrity, find your real hidden talents. We are not talking about asking yourself questions like: "Can you act?" "Can you sing?" If a traditional good singing voice were required to be a pop star, opera singers would be the bestselling artists in the world. The fact is that a large proportion of today's celebrities don't fit into the standard talent categories. So what do these people have that sets them apart? The conventional answer would be that they have the "X-factor," but that is hardly a useful explanation, so let's look at some examples.

Search for your hidden talents

Finding the X-factor in you

George Clooney started acting in 1976 but had only small parts until 1993. That's 17 years of unsuccessful struggle—so at least we can identify one handy talent for would-be celebrities right away: persistence. But let's look at more detail about what happened in 1993. Clooney had for nearly 20 years played the part of a goofy-looking, comical, screw-up. Let's be honest—Clooney is a funny guy. And that sort of comical character was probably what he felt good at, possibly even the sort of

The Clooney story

roles closest to his own personality. Then in the early 90s he started to appear in the roles of more successful, grown-up characters. For *Bodies of Evidence* he cut his hair to a length that at least didn't look entirely out of place in an office environment. And in his real breakthrough role, as Dr. Doug Ross in *ER*, not only was his hair trimmed to perfection, but his role was that of a masculine, womanizing, yet highly successful doctor. And suddenly women all over the world started to fantasize about this handsome, respectable-looking man, who only four years earlier had made women switch channels in his clown-like roles in films such as *The Return of The Killer Tomatoes*. Whether it was by coincidence or deliberate image building we may never know, but the fact is that Clooney found that his real talent was not acting; it was acting as a handsome, charming, professional gentleman. So when you are identifying your talents, don't be general. Don't just say, "I'm good at acting" or "I'm good at singing." Go into minute details. Identify exactly what you are good at, exactly what your strengths are.

The Jim Carrey story

Just for the sake of balance, let's look at a celebrity forced to move in perhaps the opposite direction of Clooney. Jim Carrey's first film role, in the 1981 film *Rubberface,* was basically as a nice, quiet young man—none of the absurd madness that he is famous for today. When you watch the movie now, you cannot help but shake your head and think "that's not Jim Carrey!" But what is obvious today, was hardly obvious back then. It took Carrey years to find his style—to identify exactly what it was that made him better than the competition—and then focus on that. In 1992 Carrey was offered the lead role in the slapstick comedy *Ace Ventura: Pet Detective* (released in 1994). But Carrey refused to take the role unless he was allowed to rewrite the script to suit his over-the-top new style. That is the sign of a celebrity genius. He had identified exactly what he was good at and was willing to risk losing his biggest role offer yet in order to build his image around those talents. In the end he was allowed to rewrite the script; the film was a huge success and Carrey's career took off so quickly NASA for a time considered harnessing its energy for a manned mission to Mars.

So, then, how do you find your hidden talent? Well, first you need to understand that what you are good at is not necessarily where your talent lies. Realizing this is crucial. Clooney was undoubtedly good at playing the role of a semi-goofy, long-haired, screw-up. But "good" isn't going to cut it if you want to reach the top. "Good," provided you are also

How to find your hidden talents

What you are good at may not be your talents

very hardworking, persistent, and a bit lucky, may bring you some small roles in a few independent films, but that's when those who are merely good will hit the wall. You need that little extra to reach the top.

A friend of mine, a French talent agent, used to say, "I'd rather work with a lousy amateur than a professional who's just good." His theory, and over the years I have come to agree with him, was that a hardworking person can become pretty good without any real talent. But then as an agent, you really don't have much to work with. In a guy just off the street, on the other hand, you may be able to find true talent, which with proper training and guidance can result in greatness.

Anyone can become good if he or she just works hard

It should be mentioned that my friend never once to my knowledge took on a "lousy amateur" as a client, so clearly he was exaggerating. But his point is important enough: You need to find your own X-factor. Working hard will never replace true talent. You may become good, but never great.

Hard work will never replace real talent

So look at what you are good at. Then ask yourself: am I good at this because I have worked really hard on it? Or am I truly talented? Don't be too hard on yourself here—I am not in any way trying to discourage you. If

Are you good at something because you have worked hard or do you really have a talent?

2: Find your real talents

you are good at something, chances are you're talented at it too. But be honest with yourself. Most people only get one shot at a career in show business, so make sure you head in the right direction from the start.

When you are pretty sure you have nailed down your general talents—be it acting, singing, dancing or writing scripts—try to go into greater depth. What sort of acting are you talented at? What sort of roles? You may have some thoughts on this already—but as we saw in the above real-life examples, it's easy to misjudge this. What you need is experience and feedback. And the only way of getting that is going out and trying your skills in front of a live audience. If it is acting you're aiming at, get as many different roles in amateur plays as possible. Try to sign up for some local amateur stand-up. You don't even have to think you're funny to try it out; sometimes you will really surprise yourself.

Be specific when identifying your talents

Try, try, and try again

Remember that there is a difference in how you are on a personal level and what you may be talented at in a professional context. Your personality has been shaped by many things outside your control, things that are often not related to your talents. Some people are extremely entertaining and fun to be with, but turn out to be brilliant dramatic actors. And vice versa: a seeming bore in personal

Your professional talent may have little to do with your personality

life may be a truly brilliant comedian in front of the camera.

Rowan Atkinson

Rowan Atkinson is often cited as an example of the potentially huge difference between on-screen and off-screen personalities. Somehow the rumor has spread that Rowan Atkinson in personal life is dull, gray, and boring. I can speak from personal experience when I say that there is absolutely no truth in this. Rowan Atkinson is, however, a very serious person who takes a great deal of pride in the technical side of humor; he treats comedy as a science, and perhaps therein lie both the key to his success and the source of the rumor. The story does illustrate well, however, that someone who may not immediately seem funny—he tends not to talk funny and make silly faces when you sit down with him to have a serious chat—may be an extremely talented comedian.

Experiment and get experience

The only way to really identify your true talents is by experimenting and getting experience. Obviously you need to work with a basic idea in the first place—don't book an ice dancing competition on Monday, a lead role in a local performance of the *Nutcracker* ballet on Tuesday, and a stand-up gig

2: Find your real talents

on Wednesday. But you should strive to get experience within your chosen profession as wide as possible and as early as possible in your career. Don't just decide from the onset that you are a good dramatic actor and try nothing else. Even if it turns out you weren't any good at certain types of roles, the experience will certainly be extremely valuable for your future career.

The wider the experience, the better the chance of finding your true talent

How to Become a Celebrity

3 STUDY HARD

3.1 Talent is not an accident of birth

So you have identified your real talent. Good! But talent is no substitute for hard work. In fact, talent usually depends on it.

Talent must be supplemented by hard work

There is no doubt that Tiger Woods has a unique talent for golf. But would he be a top player without spending hours and hours practicing very day? Of course not. No matter how gifted you are, you don't just walk out on a golf course, ask the caddie whether you grip the club on the long pointy end or the big blunt one, swing, and hit the ball 350 yards.

Tiger Woods

It is the same with acting, music, writing or whatever your chosen profession is. You think you're good at acting? Well, unless you have had years of professional training you're not. Depressing? Not at all! It's great because it means that if you are willing to work hard to achieve your goals you will have a huge advantage over those who are not.

In my experience it is the willingness to accept that you need to learn and the willingness to train hard for years and years that separate

Accept hard work as a necessity for success

those who make it from those who flip burgers for the rest of their lives.

The Brad Pitt story

Take Brad Pitt, for example. Brad Pitt moved to Los Angeles with hardly any acting experience and no training whatsoever. Hardly a recipe for success, regardless of talent. And not surprisingly, he struggled to get parts. Living in an apartment in North Hollywood together with eight friends—without any furniture except a toaster, a TV and a sleeping bag each—his life was far from the glamour he probably had envisioned.

Forced to do odd jobs at a place called the Job Factory (It's closed now but in its days it helped many a struggling actor and probably has more famous people as past employees than any other company in the world), his work included moving refrigerators and dressing up as a giant chicken for *El Pollo Loco*. One of the jobs he got was apparently driving strippers around to bachelor parties. It may not have been very glamorous, but it probably beat dressing up as a chicken. On his last day of work before he quit, he met a girl who told him about an acting class with a man named Roy London. Brad contacted London and ended up studying with him. How long do you think he studied before he was able to land a contract with a talent agent? Not three weeks, not three months, oh no. He studied under London for three years. Three years of hard study while barely scraping together a living from odd jobs. That is the sort of dedication that you often find in people who are later described as "extremely talented." Let's be honest, talent is not just an accident of birth. It is the result of very hard work for a very long period of time.

I'm in no way trying to discourage you here. If you can walk into the office of a talent agent, get an audition, and land a major role right away, then I take my hat off to you and congratulate you. But for us mere mortals, I am just trying to be realistic and prepare you for what lies ahead. Success is the result of hard work over many years. And if you want to be successful, then you must be prepared to make that investment.

Prepare for what lies ahead

3.2 Study well

Before you join any class under the sun, take a step back and ask yourself what you want to achieve. Success is a step-by-step process, so pull out a pen and paper and start writing.

What do you want to achieve?

First identify what skills you need to succeed. You want to be a famous actor? Well obviously you'll need acting skills. But that is

Success is a step-by-step process

hardly sufficient on its own. You need confidence, you need masses of audition practice to keep your nerves in place, you need people skills, and you need to be able to sell yourself well. The list goes on. It is the same for any other industry. To be a famous pianist you obviously have to be able to play the piano well. But that is not enough. You need an understanding of the pieces you are playing that only the study of music history can often give you. You need to be able to present an image that will attract people's attention, so you need some marketing skills or at least a promotion plan.

| Brainstorm for ideas | First brainstorm for some time. Write down any skill you think is required or at least helpful in achieving your overall goal. Then organize them into milestones. Focus on the fundamentals first. For an actor this will obviously be acting skills, but also stand-alone voice training, a good understanding of regional dialects and sociolects, and any other skills you think will help your acting.

Look at skills that will help you in an indirect way. I always advise a broad training in sales and marketing skills, for example. Such skills will not only help you sell yourself better, but they will also make you better at reading people's minds and understanding

Sidebar notes:
- Brainstorm for ideas
- Set milestones
- Look at skills that will help you in an indirect way

what they want. Having sales experience also helps you in controlling a conversation and achieving the results you want, often without the other party understanding that you have manipulated him or her (I used the word "manipulate" in its widest of meanings and not to indicate something negative).

<small>Learn how to be a good seller— even if you will never work in sales!</small>

Start organizing the skills into milestones. Ideally, set a date for when you want to achieve a certain level with each skill. Under each milestone start adding to-dos. Now you need to be creative. There is more than one way to learn. Sure, you can read a book about selling. It's probably a great idea to do so. But it is not a substitute for a few months' work in a good call center. "What!" you may exclaim at this point. But it is not a misprint. The road to true success is long, and you will need to earn some money on the way. So why flip burgers when there are plenty of jobs in call centers that will not only help put bread on the table, but also teach you some essential skills on the way.

<small>Set deadlines for your skill levels</small>

<small>Nothing beats real experience</small>

And acting training can also be found outside the traditional classroom. The actor and famous comedian Eddy Izzard began his career as a street performer in Covent Garden, riding the unicycle and performing handcuff escapes. Not only useful if you are arrested on DUI charges (most celebrities seem to be at one

<small>Think untraditionally</small>

point or another) but also very good training in performing in front of a live audience.

Be creative

So try to be creative in how you plan your training. When you go to an audition there will be a lot of other guys there who have taken acting classes. Your broader experience base may be what sets you apart from the rest.

I'm in no way advocating skipping the traditional classroom education. I'm just pointing out that you may add to that with some more untraditional training—and perhaps even make some money at the same time.

When you finally have your to-do list, make sure to review it the next day. Ask yourself if you have perhaps been too optimistic with your timeline. Try to make your goals and milestones hard, but realistic. There is no point in having a list where you fall behind schedule before the ink has dried.

Be realistic in your goals

Stick to your plan!

And now comes the difficult part. Stick to your plan! It's not going to be fun every day. Life just isn't. You'll have plenty of time for fun when you've made it.

To-do lists—online tools

There are some great online tools if you really want to go all the way with your to-do lists. If you really get them detailed enough, they can be a great tool for achieving success. One of my favorites is www.todoist.com where you can list your to-dos and receive reminders on email. You don't need to be Rainman to use it. If you like to work according to a plan, such websites are perfect!

If you do find yourself falling behind your schedule, try to identify why. If it is because you were too optimistic in the first place, go ahead and revise it. It is better to have a realistic plan that you can follow than an outdated list that just makes you feel like you have failed. But it you are falling behind because you haven't worked hard enough, then sit down and ask yourself what you need to do to pull yourself together. We all have times when we become unfocused or just plain lazy. It's natural. What is important is to identify it and do something about it. Break up your normal routine—skip to another item on you plan. Or just sit down and think about the success you are working toward. Envision yourself as the celebrity you will become if you work hard enough—anything to get your motivation back.

	Identify reasons for delays
	Revise deadlines if justified
	Becoming lazy?
	Work on your motivation

3.3 Study others

Learn from other people's successes and failures

Whatever challenges you are facing on your way to celebrity status, you can be sure many have faced the same issues before you. Some have failed and some have succeeded. Learning from other people's mistakes and successes can save you a lot of time and headache.

Use the Internet efficiently

Internet has made studying other celebrities incredibly easy. The amount of information that can be found within minutes through Google and other search engines is baffling. It took us less than 10 seconds to find that Brad Pitt has studied with voice coach Ron Anderson, for example. Or that Halle Berry took acting classes from Margie Haber. And as for learning from other people's mistakes?

SAG website—scam warnings

Screen Actors Guild and American Federation of Television and Radio Artists have tons of useful information about scams and a lot of useful information that will protect you from the many unscrupulous companies trying to take advantage of actors.

Use the Internet and other sources to try to identify well-known people who have been in the same situation as you before. If you are a struggling stand-up comedian, read about the careers of other stand-up comedians who were once struggling and now have made it. What did they do to skyrocket their careers? But be careful! First of all, don't believe everything you read. As the amount of information available has grown on the Internet, so has the amount of misinformation. Just because an agent or a coach claims on his website that he has worked with famous actor X and famous actress Y, it is not necessarily true. Always check more than one source. And you can also use online tools such as The Wayback Machine (http://archive.org/) to check how long a website has existed and what information the site used to have.

Don't believe everything you read

Do background checks

And don't make the mistake of thinking the way to fame and fortune is copying others. There is a substantial difference between learning from others and copying. You can get inspiration and hints that may be useful and help your career considerably—and you can find the names and contact details of useful industry people such as top coaches and agents. But if you start copying others, you are certainly heading in the wrong direction. You need to create your own personality and presence in the industry. Walking in to an agent with an exact copy of Brad Pitt's early résumé, with a Brad Pitt haircut, dressed like Brad Pitt, and talking like Brad Pitt will most likely not help your

Learn, don't copy

Create your own personality

Improve on already good ideas!

career at all. At best it might land you a job as Brad Pitt's stand-in or a body double for some shots from behind when Brad himself is busy relaxing with a drink. Not a sure road to celebrity status. Take inspiration from others—but always ask yourself, "How can I improve on this? How can I adapt this in my own way?"

4 PERSISTENCE

A friend of mine once jokingly gave me this résumé and asked me what I thought:

> Age 22 - Failed as a business manager
> Age 23 - Ran for legislature and lost badly
> Age 24 - Started a business and went bankrupt
> Age 25 - Elected to legislature
> Age 26 - Sweetheart died
> Age 27 - Had a nervous breakdown
> Age 29 - Ran for Speaker and lost
> Age 31 - Defeated for Elector
> Age 34 - Defeated for Congress
> Age 37 - Elected for Congress
> Age 39 - Defeated for Congress
> Age 46 - Defeated for Senate
> Age 47 - Defeated for Vice President
> Age 49 - Defeated for Senate again
> Age 51 - Elected President of the United States

It's the record of Abraham Lincoln—and the word "persistence" certainly springs to mind. It is an example often seen in inspirational books and it is not only perhaps overused, but also not entirely accurate.

You will need persistence to succeed

However, I decided to insert it here because it does illustrate well the most important features required in order to achieve success and celebrity status: Desire and persistence.

Be prepared for an uphill struggle!

No matter how talented you are, you should not expect to just walk into your first audition and land a lead role. And to be fair, most aspiring actors don't expect this either. What many are not prepared for, though, is the degree of struggle needed—the mountain of hindrances they will meet. The problem isn't that you don't score a role on your first audition. The problem is that you won't get an audition. You most likely won't even get an agent and the acting coach you want will tell you that regretfully she is unable to accept you as a student. And this doesn't go on for a week or a month; it goes on for years. It's enough to break all but the most persistent talent! So how do you deal with all these problems? How do you find the motivation to keep at it, to try again and again until you finally succeed?

Break down problems into smaller bits

Remember the milestones and the to-do lists? Look at all the problems you face and break them down to logical bits. You want to get a role, so you need an audition. In order to get a proper audition you need an agent; in order

4: Persistence

to get an agent you should be a SAG member; and in order to get SAG membership you will need some roles and so on and so on. If you look at the problem as a whole, it may seem overwhelming. The way to handle complex and overwhelming problems is to break them down into manageable bits. First identify the crucial steps required to move forward. For many aspiring actors, getting your first agent is the big one. Make a list of all the agents you are prepared to work with—don't aim for super-agents that in any case won't touch you unless you've got a box office hit or an Academy Award on your résumé. Find the name of some solid, good agents who are prepared to work with up-and-coming actors (see chapter 8). That in itself is a good milestone. It will require lot of research, but it is a manageable milestone. Then as the next milestone identify exactly what each of these agents will require for you to be of interest to them. That will give you some very clear milestones going forward, such as "become SAG eligible," etc. Handling each problem on its own, you will be able to see a clear way forward. It may become clear to you at this point that you've got a long road ahead of you, but at least you have a single identifiable goal to work toward at any given point. The biggest mistake I see in young aspiring actors is lack of a clear direction. Many of them work hard on their careers, but

Aim high, but not too high

Don't be a headless chicken—work toward specific goals

they are all over the place like headless chickens: a half completed acting class here, some random voice training with unknown coaches there, without any proper structure or plan.

Work on your motivation too

When you have managed to outline not only a long-term plan, but also clearly identifiable goals on the way, keeping your motivation high is going to be much easier. Even though completing a course or achieving one more credit toward you SAG membership may not seem like a big deal in itself—it won't make your life different overnight— it gives you a feeling of success. And that feeling keeps your morale high and builds your self-confidence enough to move even further forward. Proper career planning like this gives you a massive advantage over competing actors who just run around town randomly throwing about their résumés and portfolios.

Break down your success targets into smaller simple targets to keep morale high

Proper career planning gives you the edge over your competitors!

Persistence is something that you build

So persistence isn't just a character trait you're born with; it is something that you build through proper career and goal management. But realize that no amount of talent and planning can alter the fact that the road to success is long and hard. There are going to be days when you start doubting your choice, when you have been struggling for years, and your friends suddenly are

How do you keep focused on your goals?

4: Persistence

completing their educations and are starting to have careers and proper jobs—with proper salaries. So what can you do to keep positive and focused when life in general seems to have conspired against you?

First of all, you need to be mentally prepared. If you realize at an early stage that there will be days when you feel like giving up, you can take actions to keep yourself going even through the heaviest of days. A trick I used in my early career was to take 15 minutes on my good days—when I had a lot of positive energy—and write down why I had chosen this career. I would write down all the positive things about what I was doing, both the good things here and now (living in an exciting place, hanging out with creative guys, having a lot of freedom in my day-to-day life) and the great things I was working toward. I used to seal the letter in an envelope and then open it on a bad day. It is amazing how the positive energy I had felt when I wrote the letter helped lift me up when I read it weeks or even months later. I used to think of it as storing some of the positive energy away from the best of days and using it to recharge myself on the worst of days.

Be prepared for a struggle

Keep positive reminders for yourself

Secondly, don't be afraid of talking to people when you are down. Talking openly to a friend (preferably one who is not too

Talk to people

depressed himself) or even a professional such as a coach or psychologist can help you look at problems in a different way. Every problem has a solution, but often it takes a third party to see it when things are really looking bad.

Move milestones around, but don't take breaks when you are down

Finally, don't be afraid to shuffle things around on your list of milestones. Some people like to take a break to "recharge their batteries." I have never advocated this myself. I have seen so many struggling actors go back to their families in the middle of a depression "just for a few days to get some energy back," and very few of them returned. The problem doesn't go away while you are away, and traveling back to face them may suddenly seem very, very hard. Take your breaks when you're on a high and work hard when you're on a low.

Problems must be solved, not avoided

5 BUILDING AN IMAGE

5.1 How to find your own image

It is pretty obvious that building the right image is essential for any celebrity. But exactly what is part of a celebrity's image? An image is more than what you do and how you look. It is how you are perceived by people. So how do you build the right image?

> An image is more than what you do and how you look

First let's look at what you want to achieve with your image. If you are reading this book you obviously want to gain celebrity status. And when you do, you want to make sure you remain in the limelight and you obviously want to be able to capitalize on your celebrity status.

Changing your image—the public perception of you—can be almost impossible. So you want to make sure you build an image that helps you achieve all your goals right from the start. Many short-lived celebrities have made the mistake of building an image only suitable for getting them into the limelight, but not for keeping them there.

> Changing your image is hard—get it right from the start!

> *I don't want to ridicule or criticize specific celebrities. But for the sake of*

> Tara Reid

illustration I will mention the, so far at least, somewhat disappointing career of Tara Reid, simply because it is a classic example of a career built with an image that was very difficult to capitalize on. After the success with American Pie and American Pie 2 it seemed almost unthinkable that she would nearly disappear from the limelight within a few years. But when she first got into the limelight it was without any proper image—apart from mediocre acting and a bit of partying. And those are hardly traits suitable for a long-term career. And when the limelight faded, instead of taking a step back and rebuilding her career properly, panic measures to bring media attention to herself took the form of scandalous behavior: wild partying, wardrobe malfunctions (apparently the technical name for showing yourself topless accidentally on purpose) and finally the death of any proper celebrity status: a quick in-and-out of the Big Brother House. She was seemingly never advised to build an image that catered to what the people and the media want. As we discussed in chapter 1 there is a difference between being famous and being a real celebrity. In order to be a celebrity you must be likable enough for people to feel a relationship with you. And on this point Tara failed miserably—at least so far. You might get to be well-known as an out-of-control drunk, but it is not an image you can capitalize on.

| An image must get you into the limelight—and keep you there

If you're image is only good for getting you into the limelight, but not keeping you there, then why bother? If you just want to have 15 minutes of fame, there are easier ways than spending years building a Hollywood career.

When you do plan your public image, make sure it caters to the needs of people as discussed in chapter 1. Make sure you are exciting and glamorous enough to be a substitute for the excitement most people miss in their lives and make sure you give people something they want to gossip about, not just once, but again and again. You can be scandalous, but don't be predictable: people may run to their neighbors to tell them they saw the preacher with a bottle of whiskey, but they won't bother to say they saw a drunken alcoholic. Finally you must make sure people feel a connection with you; they must somehow see a little of themselves in you.

| Add excitement to people's lives

| Don't be predictable

Never try to reinvent yourself completely. No one can keep up playing someone else for years, being someone else every time they go out of the house.

| Never try to reinvent yourself completely

> Focus on being yourself, but with a twist

I always advise people to focus on being themselves. But try to look critically at the image you portray as seen from the outside. Check that image against the guidelines I have outlined here. And make sure you portray a uniform image—don't try to be everything at the same time. You may be a complex person—most people are—but complexity doesn't go well with modern media. Keep your image simple and it will be much more effective.

> Your focus is to be great at what you do

And never, ever forget: Your primary focus should always be on being great at what you do. True and lasting fame comes mostly from great skills.

5.2 Changing your name

> Changing your name is usually easy, but the procedure varies from state to state

In most countries changing your name is actually quite easy from a legal perspective. In the majority of US states you simply need to fill in a petition stating your reason for wanting to change your name. This petition is submitted to a judge and the name change will almost always be approved as long as your new name doesn't imply a "fraudulent intent," violate a trademark, or use obscene words. In the UK it is even easier: all you have to do is complete a Deed Poll and your change of name is legally binding.

> Don't change your name on a whim

But even if the legal process is simple, changing your name is something that shouldn't be taken easy. You need to carefully consider if a change is necessary and if so, you also need to consider your new name very thoroughly. If you are in the early stages of your career, try the name you are considering at a few auditions to see what kind of reaction you get. And do proper research to make sure no other professional is using the same name.

Change your name only for a good reason

In general, however, I always advise my clients to stick to their real name (or simplified versions of the same) unless there is a specific reason to change.

5.2.1 STAGE NAMES

Instead of actually changing your name, you may consider just taking a stage name or a "nom de plume" if you are trying to break through as a writer. Stage names are so common in show business that SAG and other unions will require you to register both your legal name and a professional name; they can of course be the same. Usually an actor will work under a professional name that is a simplified version of his or her own name, dropping middle names or using a common nickname like Bill instead of William.

Stage names are common in show business and do not require change of legal name

SAG requires a stage name

> *If your stage name is similar to your given name, don't change your legal name*

Whether you change your legal name or just use a professional name is up to you. If you are considering a completely different name and you are early in your career, I would normally recommend a change of legal name. But if you are just using a professional name very similar to your own, there really is no need for a name change. Just make sure you fill in all forms—like employment contracts—properly (they will usually have a field called "credited as") or you may have a problem with such things as cashing your paychecks later.

> *Check employment contracts and make sure your legal name is correct!*

5.2.2 NAMES THAT ARE DIFFICULT TO PRONOUNCE OR SPELL

Some names are just plain difficult to pronounce or spell. You will know that you have such a name if throughout your childhood when your name was being read out, there was a long pause and then the reader tried three different versions of your name—all of them wrong—and finally just mumbled something. Or if every time you try to book a ticket on the phone the operator goes, "Um, could you repeat that?" and then you go through a ten-minute process of saying, "no, not b, g. Like 'golf.'"

> *A little uniqueness is fine, but a name should be easy to remember*

Such names may be beautiful and impressive. And a little bit of uniqueness is fine; it makes the name more memorable. But there is a

5: Building an image

limit. If your name is just too difficult to pronounce, it may be a hindrance to your career.

The singer Maria Callas is an example of a celebrity who changed her name for such a reason. Her name used to be Maria Kalogeropoulos. It is hard to imagine her having the same success with that name. Another example is Demetria Gene Guynes, or Demi Moore as you probably know her.

5.2.3 YOU SHARE YOUR NAME WITH ANOTHER CELEBRITY

This is a situation where you really should consider changing your name. Regardless of what industry you are trying to break into, if your name is Julia Roberts or Brad Pitt, you will have a problem. Change your name or use a stage name; there really is no other option.

> If you share a name with another celebrity, you usually must use a stage name or change your name

SAG will not allow two actors working under the same name— though they will allow you to use your birth name even if someone else is already working under that name. Michael Keaton, for example, could have worked under his real name of Michael Douglas. But it would hardly have been a good career move.

> Michael Keaton was born Michael Douglas

It is said that Julia Roberts was really born Julie Roberts and changed her name to Julia because there already was a Julie

Roberts registered with SAG. As far as I know the story is one of those Internet myths that sadly tend to appear when people are allowed to freely edit sites considered authoritative in their field, like Wikipedia and IMDb. Before anyone can correct it, the rumor has spread, and five years later it is cited as a fact.

5.2.4 YOUR NAME DOESN'T MATCH YOUR IMAGE

Your name should not conflict with the image you want

A very common reason for up-and-coming performers to change their names is that their current names simply don't match the images for which they are looking.

When you hear someone's name you immediately create a mental image of how that person is going to look and what sort of personality he or she will have. Some names are fairly neutral in the sense that we get no particular vibes when we hear them. James, Peter, John—names like that can fit almost anyone. But then there are certain names that immediately make you think of a stereotype. Jolene, Darlene, Sharlene, Amber, Crystal, Brandy, Shauna, and Tonya sounds like the staff list of a rundown strip club.

Some names are neutral; some names give associations to certain personalities

"Stripper names"

If you happen to be blessed with one of these or other names I may mention

5: Building an image

here, please take no offense. You may be a very intelligent person from an affluent background. I am merely pointing out how some names are perceived by a majority of people. It is useful information if you are planning a career in show business.

If you are expecting dinner guests named Olga and Bertha, and you have not met them before, you may consider making some extra large portions. Edwina, Bianca, and Wilhelmina are girls you don't want to arm wrestle with. Some people might get nervous when they learn that their surgeon is named Chip or Chad. And a pilot named Bobby Joe is just wrong.

"Russian names"

"Butch names"

"Redneck names"

The list is long of celebrities who have changed their names because they didn't match the image they wanted the public to have of them. Archibald Alexander Leach just doesn't sound as cool and masculine as Cary Grant. And Marion Morrison is hardly as good a name for a sheriff as John Wayne.

Cary Grant was born Archibald Alexander Leach

I always prefer when my clients stick to their real names. But as we have discussed, building your public image is extremely important and certain names just give people the wrong impression. If you want to be a modern stand-up comedian and your name is Albert Adolf von Muckenfuss, I probably would agree that a change in your name might help your career.

<small>Build your new name from bits of the old</small>

If you do change your name, try to build something from your old name if you can. It usually makes it easier for yourself and your friends and family to adapt to the change and just gives a less "made-up" feel. Greta Garbo is not that far from her original Greta Gustafsson. Nicolas Cage and Nicolas Coppola are not worlds apart. Luke Perry may sound much cooler, but the change from Coy Luther Perry III is a minor one. Some celebrities just dropped their last names and replaced them with their middle names, like Lea Michele Sarfati becoming just Lea Michele. The technique can be very effective and it gives you a new name that you truly feel comfortable with.

5.2.5 YOUR NAME SOUNDS TOO FOREIGN

<small>Some names sound foreign by nature</small>

This used to be considered a good reason for changing your name. Hollywood actors and actresses were considered American icons, and names that sounded too foreign were not good. Frederick Austerlitz, for example, was not the sort of name that got you roles during the 1930s and 1940s. Fred Astaire, on the other hand, sounded much less foreign.

In today's much more globalized world, I personally feel this is much less of a problem. If your name sounds foreign, but still meets the other criteria mentioned here, I would normally not advise you to change it.

Foreign names are more common than they used to be

It's still being done, though. Natalie Hershlag, for example, was probably right to change her name to Natalie Portman. But the real reason here was perhaps not that it sounded too foreign, but that it was both difficult to spell and pronounce, and a name pronounced "her slag" may also possibly not have been entirely in line with the image she wanted, at least not in Great Britain.

5.3 Your name is your trademark

So you have finally decided on a stage name and you may even have registered it with SAG or another union to make sure you can use it professionally. That should be enough, right? Well, have a look at this:

Trademarking your name is common among celebrities

> Trademark Serial Number 4134422: BRAD PITT. Entertainment services, namely, acting services (...)
>
> Trademark Serial Number 85272938: CHARLIE SHEEN. Entertainment ser-

48 | How to Become a Celebrity

vices, namely, providing motivational speakers, acting services (...)

Trademark Serial Number 77983418: MILEY CYRUS. Musical sound recordings; musical video recordings; pre-recorded CDs, DVDs (...)

United States Patent and Trademark Office

These are just some random selections from the United States Patent and Trademark Office. These celebrities haven't gone through the trouble of registering their names as trademarks just for fun!

A trademark identifies services of one seller from those of others

A trademark is a word, phrase, symbol or design, or a combination of these, identifying and distinguishing goods or services of one seller from those of others, and indicating the source of the goods and services. Names of people and companies, business logos and symbols, and particular sounds can all be trademarked. Everything from Britney Spears' name, the Nike "swoosh" logo, and the NBC chimes are registered as trademarks. Trademarks identify a product, service, person, or thing from others in the same field, and trademark infringement has, and always will be, a serious offense.

A stage name registered with your union does NOT give trademark protection

Just because you have managed to register your stage name with your union and used it in a few productions does not prevent anyone

5: Building an image

else from setting up a website and selling shampoo, shoes, perfume, or dog clothes in your name! However, if you have registered your name with the Patent and Trademark Office, you will be able to prevent such infringements of your trademark.

A particular problem of the times is domain names. A lot of people speculate in setting up domains with famous names, either to sell dubious products or for fraudulent purposes. You can, and should, register your domain as soon as you have decided on a stage name. But even if you have registered YourName.com, someone will always be able to find an available domain name such as YourName.me, Your-Name.com, etc. Having a trademark protection will put you in a strong position to fight such infringements. Even if the domain name is not exactly the same as your name or trademark, your protection extends to anything that is confusingly similar, even if it isn't exactly the same.

Domain names

Register your domain, but remember that there are endless domain name possibilities

Register your trademark as soon as you feel you can afford to do so. If you wait too long, someone may beat you to the mark. And always use a law firm when registering your trademark. Even if it can be done more cheaply online, a lawyer will be able to help you identify exactly what goods and services

Don't wait too long

you should register your trademark for, and in general make sure you receive maximum protection from your registration.

6 GET NOTICED

It goes without saying that you have to be seen to be a celebrity. If people don't notice you, you may be a good actor or performer, and you may still have a great career, but you won't enjoy celebrity status.

Fame can come in many different shapes and forms

Fame can come in many different shapes and forms. Theodore Edward Hook—not very well known today, but famous in the first half of the 19th century—once made a bet with the architect and playwright Samuel Beazley. Apparently Beazley had been complaining that it was very hard designing a building that people would actually take notice of and talk about. Hook replied that it was nonsense and that he could make any house in London famous. To prove it he picked the most mundane house he could think of, 54 Berners Street, and told Beazley he could make it the most talked of address in London within a week. The next morning Hook started writing hundreds of letters requesting deliveries, visitors, and assistance to the house. On November 27, 1810, at five o'clock in the morning, a sweep arrived to sweep the chimneys. The maid who answered the door informed him that no

The 54 Berners Street story

sweep had been requested, and that his services were not required. But before she had finished the sentence, another sweep presented himself, then another, and another, twelve in all. While the poor maid was trying to deal with the rather surprising onslaught of chimney sweeps, a fleet of carts carrying large deliveries of coal began to arrive, followed by a series of cake-makers delivering large wedding cakes, lawyers, then doctors and vicars summoned to minister to someone in the house they had been told was dying. Over the next hours deliveries of tons of fish, over a dozen pianos, and a steady stream of shoemakers appeared at the door, "along with six stout men bearing an organ" and a coffin "made to measure five feet six, sixteen." By lunchtime the house was on everybody's lips, and the city buzzed with rumors of foreign royals and wealth beyond belief. Dignitaries, including the Governor of the Bank of England, the Duke of York, the Archbishop of Canterbury, and the Lord Mayor of the City of London also arrived. The narrow streets became congested with tradesmen and onlookers, and by early evening large parts of London had been brought to a standstill.

The owner of the house, a Mrs. Tottenham, who had nothing to do with the hoax, cer-

6: Get noticed

tainly became famous. But it was hardly a fame she could capitalize on. On the contrary, she is said to have had a nervous breakdown and had to be sent off for convalescence.

I included the story to show that if someone could make a dull London house famous within a day 200 years ago, then certainly anyone can gain fame quickly in today's news-driven, multimedia, Twitter and Youtube-focused world. But there is hardly any point in doing so unless you can gain a fame that you can capitalize on, a fame that you can use to build a long career.

<small>Fame can come quickly in today's Internet-driven world</small>

When you actively seek publicity it should as a general rule always be in connection with your work. Not only does this help build your career, but it also helps you avoid the trap of seeming desperate.

<small>Seek fame in connection to your work</small>

Ideally your work should speak for itself. Having said that, however, it is important to note that even brilliant work is often overlooked unless you do something to make the media take notice. If you have advanced far enough in your career to work with some of the major players in your industry, they will certainly take care of a lot of the publicity for you. But if you are not yet at that stage, you need to do a lot of the work yourself.

Don't do stunts on your own if you are part of a production

Whenever you are planning some publicity stunts for a production or a project you have been involved in, make sure you organize it together with the project team. The director of the independent wartime drama you just starred in may perhaps not feel that your parachuting naked from the Empire State Building matched entirely with his own planned promotions. But never be afraid of bringing specific ideas to the table even if your role in a project has been a minor one.

Start with websites, blogs, Twitter, and Facebook

In addition to publicity for projects you have been involved in, you obviously also need to build your own image through the media. New media, like websites and blogs, Twitter and Facebook, are perfect tools for presenting yourself to the world and building fans and followers. You should start using such tools early on in your career and always use any opportunity to promote them.

> *New publicity channels like blogs, Twitter, and Facebook also carry some specific dangers of which you need to be aware. First of all, remember to keep your sites or accounts active. There is nothing more depressing than a Twitter account where the last tweet was three years ago, or a blog that stopped being updated in 2006. If you fail to keep your online presence*

6: Get noticed

exciting and interesting, it can actually work against you. Second, always remember that what has been put online stays online. Those semi-nude party pictures from four years back may not be so good when you are being considered for a role as a quiet, shy girl in a historical drama. You might be able to remove stupid comments and embarrassing pictures, but chances are someone will find a record of it somewhere. Search engines store pages; removing things from cyber history has proven very, very difficult indeed. And third, always, always think before you tweet or comment on anything. 50 Cent's tsunami tweet "Wave will hit 8am them crazy white boys gonna try to go surfing" was not a winner. And Gilbert Gottfried's "I just split up with my girlfriend, but like the Japanese say, there'll be another one floating by any minute now" tweeted during the same tsunami disaster cost him his job as the Aflac Duck voice.

> Be aware of the danger of immediate mass communication
>
> Things don't go away online
>
> 50 Cent's tsunami tweet

In whatever you do, whether it is offline publicity stunts, a post on your Facebook account, or a short tweet, make sure it is in line with the overall image you wish to present. If you are trying to build an image of yourself as a hardworking, serious actress, a tweet about how hung over you are feeling may not be

> Make sure what you do is in line with your image

the thing. And opposite if you're trying to present yourself as a fun-loving up-and-coming stand-up comedian, a tweet about the socioeconomic consequences of the war in Afghanistan may not hit the target market.

Be original

When planning pure publicity stunts, make sure you stay seemingly original. Do feel free to take inspiration from others, but do it in your own way. Before Jackass, jumping off buildings dressed as Superman, swimming with alligators, or snorkeling in sewers may have been just the thing to create a Youtube hit. These days, though, not so much.

Youtube

Don't get me wrong; there is still a lot you can do with Youtube, and uploading videos there can be a fantastic way of getting massive attention without much capital investment. New videos go viral day. But make sure whatever you do is original and in line with your image, or the whole thing will just backfire badly.

Hang with the right crowd

Never underestimate the importance of hanging with the right crowd. Not only will being seen with the right people at the right places help build your important network of contacts, but it may be a good way of getting noticed by the public too.

6: Get noticed

Finally a word of warning against journalists. Journalists are extremely important in building a career. You need them as much as they need you. But remember that they are not there to help you. They are there to sell newspapers and magazines and get high ratings for their TV shows. Keep that in mind when you talk to them, and remember that the spin they put on a story may not be the spin you wanted. When you expected "up-and-coming actor in naked parachute to support animal rights," the headline might end up as "drunken wannabe actor in naked rampage on rooftop" if they think it will sell more papers.

Journalists have a job to do—and it is not to help you

Before you start giving any formal interviews, you should make sure you have had a few training sessions with people who know how the media works. It can be a friend, an agent, or even a specialist in media interview training.

Train for interview situations

> *A few general hints before an interview: Always, always prepare well. Try to think through any possible question they may ask. Before the interview you should decide on a clear message you want to get across. If you don't know why you are doing the interview, then it is unlikely it will go as you hope. You should also—*

Always prepare well for interviews

and if you're an actor you will know this already—always watch your body language. Practice interviews at home in front of a camera so you know beforehand where you want to keep your hands, how much forward or backward you should lean, etc. Learning during the interview will never make you look good. In order to control the interview you need to know how to bridge, that is forcing the conversation from one topic to another in a natural way. You will learn more about that as part of the selling techniques in chapter 7. And finally; always remember that nothing is ever "off the record"!

> Practice interview situations in front of a camera

> Try to control the interview by using techniques from this book

6.1 Get involved with people in the industry

Let's face it—you can't just pick up the phone and call George Lucas. Building a network in your chosen industry is like building a house. You don't start with the roof. You start with the foundation. Building the foundation may not be the most exciting part of the job, but a rock solid foundation is crucial. Start locally. If you're embarking on an acting career, start with your local amateur theatres and join some acting classes. It may feel like a long way from Hollywood (unless you happen,

> Build a network

> Start locally

of course, to be living there), but you will be surprised by how many in the business who have a friend who knows someone who happens to be an agent or a talent scout or works for a production company. When you have a solid local base, start building your broader network.

Don't be afraid to ask for introductions. Show people your talent, but don't be afraid to also show that you have ambitions. You may not be lucky enough to get a straight introduction to some Hollywood hotshot, but don't panic. At this stage you need to build your network one step at the time. The director of your local amateur theatre may not know Steven Spielberg or Oliver Stone, but he may know the director of a professional theatre in a bigger city or an acting teacher in California.

Ask for introductions

When you do get a promise of an introduction, make the most of it. Here we move into selling skills (good selling is really just about getting the result you want), which I discuss in depth in chapter 7. But we'll look at some good strategies for introductions right away:

Be pushy but not rude

Get a clear promise. People may be a little hesitant about introducing you to an important friend, particularly if you have gotten a bit ahead of yourself and asked before you know

Get a clear promise

them well. At the same time people in general aim to please, at least if you ask nicely. If so, they may give you a very vague promise, like "sure, I'll mention you to him" or "I'll send you his contact details." Protective answers like this are only natural and shouldn't be taken in any negative way. But they don't do you much good either. Getting the contact details for an agent that could easily be found online or in the Yellow Pages is not a proper introduction. You need to press them for more. Smile and answer positively: "That's great! I really appreciate it." But don't stop there. What you want is for your friend to actually introduce you to this important person. That means that he or she actual contacts this person and mentions you. Only that will be seen as an endorsement of your skills and talents. Be careful not to ask for too much up-front, but try to follow up with something like, "This is really kind of you! Could you send him an email and copy me in, just quickly introducing me?" A direct question like that is really difficult to answer in the negative. Nine out of ten times, people will feel obliged to say "Yes." They may not do it immediately, but now you have the promise and you need to use that promise by following up on it until they actually deliver. Don't be shy here. If someone promised to introduce you and then didn't do something for a few days, that doesn't mean they don't want to do

> Ideally the introduction should be direct

it. This may be very important to you, but to them it probably isn't. Just keep asking nicely "about that introduction you promised." If nothing happens and eventually it becomes clear they won't deliver on their promise, you can always offer them a way out by simply asking for the contact details so you can call the person yourself. At least you're no worse off than if you hadn't asked for the introduction in the first place!

Take what you can get

So, what else can you do to build your network from the ground up? Well, introductions from people in the trade can work well even when it is to a person neither of you know! Imagine you're an agent, a talent scout, or a director—or anyone important in your chosen industry. Most likely you get a lot of letters starting with "Hi, my name is (...)" Unless the next words are "Angelina Jolie" the letter is most likely heading for the trashcan or the big pile of similar letters that his secretary has been intending to read for the last 18 months. Then imagine receiving something like this:

Introductions to third parties / references / endorsements

> Dear Sir,
>
> My name is Peter Jones and I am the director of the Wellheaven Theatre. I'm writing to you to introduce one of our most talented young actresses, Jane Doe.

> *Although Jane is only 16, she has truly impressed all of us here at Wellheaven Theatre with her talent, hard work, and dedication...*

Which one do you think goes in the trash and which one do you think he or she takes the time to read? It may not immediately result in a callback. But you are getting your name out there in a good way. Eventually it will pay off.

Remember: your foundation must be rock solid

Now, hopefully, you are beginning to see why a rock solid foundation of solid, ordinary contacts in the business is extremely important. We have used acting-related examples above, but the industry doesn't matter; the principle is the same. You want to become a model? Get in touch with local photographers. Perhaps even upmarket local clothes shops—they often arrange fashion shows or viewings for loyal customers or at the local mall for special occasions. And if you are trying to break into the music industry, your local radio station is a great place to start.

7 BECOME A SELLER

7.1 Why do you need to know sales techniques

It may seem odd that I keep referring to the importance of learning basic sales skills when you presumably have absolutely no plans of becoming a seller. But think about it. What is selling really, except making people do what you want? Sales technique is all about gently manipulating people to do what you want them to do. Whether it is buying a new photocopier, giving you a role in a movie, or giving you a stand-up gig doesn't really matter. The techniques you can use to achieve your goals are the same.

Why learn sales techniques?

Do not underestimate how much having good selling skills can influence your results and your career. Anyone who has worked a day in a call center, worked with stock brokers, or just listened to a really good seller work his magic will know that proper sales skills can mean the difference between living your dream life and flipping burgers at McDonald's. (If flipping burgers at McDonald's is your dream life, then obviously you're lucky—you can skip this part).

Never underestimate what good sales skills can do for any career

So, can anyone become a great seller? Yes and no. Like anything else in life, personal talent obviously plays a part. But I know from personal experience that with proper training and practice, anyone—regardless of talent—can become a pretty good seller. More than good enough to make a huge difference to your career.

Anyone can learn basic sales techniques

7.2 Preparation

As with everything else in life, preparation is the foundation for good selling. It doesn't matter if you are going to an audition, a meeting with an acting coach you really hope will accept you as a student at a discounted rate, or a job interview. You need to prepare or you will fail. Don't just prepare for the professional aspect, your acting skills for an audition, for example. Prepare the sales pitch too.

Don't just prepare for the job; prepare how you will sell yourself

Make sure you have decided on exactly what you want to achieve when making a phone call or going into a meeting. Keep that goal in mind at all times. Everything you say and do should be about controlling the phone call or meeting toward that goal. You will learn some techniques to do this in this chapter.

Know what you want to achieve

7: Become a seller

Always write a sales pitch down on a piece of paper. It doesn't matter if you're not going to follow it in the end (although you always should try). Writing a pitch down will force you to think through what needs to be in place for you to close a deal and in what order you should progress.

Always write down a sales pitch, even if you won't use it

Some days you just need to get on the phone and call people, calling agents and casting directors, for example. (It's a sensitive issue, but sometimes a bit of active phone marketing is required.) It can be a real struggle getting going on a day like that, particularly if you don't feel too comfortable selling yourself on the phone. Do all your preparatory work the day or evening before your call day. If you are going to start looking up phone numbers and putting together a call list after you have begun your workday, you will find that pretty soon the whole day has disappeared. Preparation saves time and maximizes your opportunities for a successful day of contacts and closes. It also removes any excuses you may try to come up with for not doing something you feel uncomfortable doing. The day before you should organize your call lists and workspace. And you need to have set some specific goals and have prioritized your call times.

Get started early by being well prepared

Preparation saves time and maximizes your success rate

Set high goals

As for your call goals, always set a target that is twice as high as you would think possible to get through. You will soon enough find out that 70% of all calls end up on voicemail or with a message left with a secretary.

Start the day with some easy calls. A callback to someone you have spoken to before or a thank you call to someone who has helped you in some way. It gets the day off to a good, positive start.

The value of thank you calls

While we are at it, thank you calls are a much undervalued sales technique. If someone has helped you in one way or another—whether he or she has asked you in for an audition, offered you a job or just given you a contact number—make a call to say thanks. It is a really good way not only to seem professional, but also get some more favor out of him or her.

> In the most professional call centers, this technique is used to great effect by top sellers. Making a thank you call distinguishes these sellers from their competitors and gives a very professional impression. A lot of those calls are just what is known in the call center business as "thanks and runs," basically just "Mr. Henderson, I just wanted to thank you for

referring me to John, the casting director at Mad Studios." But sometimes you will get a positive response and you may find the person suddenly giving you more referrals or useful information and suggestions. The good thing about thank you calls is that they are now so rare that most people are taken by surprise, so getting your foot in the door is never a problem.

Get your foot in the door

7.3 The sales process

The sales process should be a one-way street toward your ultimate goal. Before you go into the meeting or lift up the phone, you will already have decided on what you want to achieve with the conversation. To achieve this goal you need to 1) get your foot in the door (this is particularly difficult when cold calling), then you need to 2) take control of the conversation, 3) remove any obstacles, and finally 4) close the deal. Below I will go through each phase separately.

Take control

Remove obstacles
Close the deal

7.3.1 Getting your foot in the door

Getting your foot in the door (literally in an office or metaphorically on the phone) is the classic problem for any seller. A lot has been written about how to do this, and I won't

An invitation saves time

go into too much detail here. But I will say this: in my experience the best way of getting your foot in the door is to be invited in first. It sounds obvious, but for one reason or other so many people—both professional sellers and others—forget this. By preparing well, you can change a potential cold call to an invitation.

Using referrals

First of all, you should always look for a way of getting a referral. A referral changes the aspect of the initial phase of the call completely. How much easier is the start, "Robert, hi, this is Joe Anderson. Peter Johnson at Smurfy Agencies suggested I call you about your upcoming audition," than a complete cold call?

Be smart when cold calling

If you really have to make a complete cold call, you should always try to include a reference to something noteworthy about the customer or his company. "Mr Robertson, this is Joe Anderson. I have been informed that you are currently looking for an actor for a new movie for Smurfy Studios and I'd like to speak with you regarding arranging an audition." It may not be ideal, but it is a good solid start. By referring to something you know about his or her current work, you grab the attention and make the person focus. It is unlikely he or she will hang up immediately.

Regardless of what strategy you chose for your initial contact, expect to meet some objections very quickly. You can read about objection handling strategies in chapter 7.3.5.

7.3.2 TAKING CONTROL OF THE CONVERSATION

A good seller controls the call without your knowing that he is doing it. He doesn't force the conversation and he definitely doesn't seem pushy or rude.

Keep the conversation under control

The easiest way to control a conversation is by asking questions. If you end a sentence with a question, people will almost always automatically answer it rather than saying what they were planning to say a second before (usually something involving being "very busy right now").

Control through questions

Using questions to control a call toward your ultimate goal is the only way you can hope to achieve what you want. No—absolutely no—sentence should come out of your mouth without a question at the end unless you are absolutely positive the caller is agreeing with you and is doing the closing for you.

End every sentence with a question

"John, I understand you are looking for someone to do a short stand-up gig on Fridays" is NOT a question. It doesn't force

Avoid early rejections at all cost

John subconsciously to answer in a specific way. If John is busy or simply doesn't know you, this is where John will answer, "Yes, but right now I'm really busy." And if you get a rejection like that early on it the call, you're screwed. "John, I understand you are looking for someone to do a short stand-up gig on Fridays. This is for the Blue Whale restaurant you run down on Elm Street, right?" That IS a question. Now subconsciously John will forget what he was going to say nine out of ten times and answer, "Yes," or "No, it's for the Blue Frog." The actual answer doesn't matter—you will be positive in either case. "Oh! I know the Blue Frog. Peter Dale who is a good friend of mine used to do gigs for you there a few years back. It's on Church Street, isn't it?" Right on to a new question.

Clear questions force an answer

Use harmless and gentle questions like this to get the call through the critical first 30 seconds. But make sure the questions are relevant! Never ask, "How's the weather there?" even if you are talking to someone on the other side of the world. Stick to questions for which you know the answer or where the answer doesn't matter. If you ask questions like, "How's business?" you may make the other person feel uncomfortable or even worse, you'll get a reply that make closing later impossible. "Not too good, I'm afraid.

Stay relevant

7: Become a seller

We had to dismiss the guy doing the Friday stand-up gig," is going to make it difficult for you to close...

When you are pretty sure you have managed to get your foot in the door, move on through your pitch. Guide the call step-by-step toward a close. In the above example you would follow up with sentences like "I have a very wide experience in stand-up comedy and have done several gigs for the Red Tiger and The Orange Orange. What sort of style are you interested in for the Blue Frog?" Again, note the question. You have presented yourself and made it obvious why you are calling, but it is too early to try to go for a close now. Ask clear questions to make sure you don't get an "I'm busy" reply at this point.

Guide the call step-by-step toward a close

Keep asking questions

Continue like this, remaining positive and proactive. And again stay relevant. "Yes, a lot of the work I have done has been very family-oriented. The Red Tiger, as you know, is a typical family restaurant too. Do you know Brian, the manager there?" Again note the question at the end. Here you are moving toward a closing. If you are lucky, he may know Brian and you will have a perfect opportunity to close. If not (and I know asking questions that may be answered "no" is considered bad sales tech-

Remain positive and proactive

niques, but sometimes you have no choice), then just try to close in a different way. If you have prepared properly you may know that this guy works in the restaurant every night. If so, you may want to try something like, "You're going to be in the restaurant a bit later today, right?" It's a direct question, but if asked at the right time, it is very difficult to reply "No."

Use data from your preparation

For the closing, always make sure you are extremely clear about what you want. First of all, a half-hearted close is not going to be worth much to you, and secondly it will seem like you have something to hide. Never just say "Great! Perhaps I can come down and have a chat with you." You're not looking for a chat. Be more direct: "Great! It certainly sounds like a gig that I would be perfect for! I can come down today to talk to you and show you some of my routines. What time would be best for you? I can be there around 5 or 6?" It's very, very direct. But in my opinion it stays on the right side of rude. And it is very, very difficult to give a "no" answer since it really doesn't fit into the question you asked. If he does say anything other than what time is best for him, it will make him seem rude—and most people will try to avoid that.

Be clear about what you want when you are closing

People in general will try to be nice

7.3.3 IDENTIFYING PERSONALITIES

We've all had the experience of making a phone call or having a meeting that we're really not looking forward to, whether it is with a difficult customer, a casting director, or someone else who might be expected to be very difficult to talk to. But then seconds after you start talking to each other, you realize that "Hey, this guy is really easy to talk to!" And there is the opposite experience of meeting a person that you think will be really nice to talk to, and then realizing that "Shit, this isn't going well at all"

Some personalities match

This happens all the time, but what is interesting—and what can really help your career—is realizing why it happens. The fact is that some people just talk well together, and others don't. But since no one can make a career out of just talking with people with a matching personality, we need to understand how to adapt to different people and different situations. Some people are better at this than others, but it is a skill that you can learn through a theoretical approach and a bit of practice. And if you have chosen an acting career, this is a good chance for some everyday acting practice too!

You must adapt to sell

Sales and sales psychology books tend to divide people into groups based on their personality and behavior in a meeting situation.

Types of personalities

The number of groups varies wildly from just two to over twenty in some literature. This book isn't about theoretical selling, though. It is about learning enough sales skills to actively manipulate a conversation to go the way you want, and for that purpose I have always found that it is sufficient to talk about three main types of behavioral patterns. Nearly anyone you talk to, on the phone or in a meeting, will fit into one of these categories.

The Energetic personality

Let's start with the group that I personally have always found the easiest to talk to: **the Energetic Guy**. The Energetic Guy has a high energy level and usually an optimistic view of life. You all know what sort of people I'm talking about—they will talk a lot, often at a very fast pace. Their positive attitude makes them very easy to talk to, but also a constant source of disappointment. If you have ever worked in a sales organization you will have heard a million times sellers say, "He didn't buy today, but this guy is definitely going to buy!" And if you have ever had a meeting with an Energetic Guy, whether it is to discuss a project, a role or a gig, you will come out feeling really good about the meeting, thinking the deal is as good as in the box. Somehow, however, it rarely is with the Energetic Guy—at least not unless you know how to handle him.

Talks a lot

The Energetic Guy usually has a problem with time management; he has a problem with promising too much, and he has a problem with just forgetting the whole thing. So when you are dealing with an Energetic Guy, you really want to make sure you are organized for him. And you want to tie him down there and then—you want to make sure his promises are clear and, if at all possible, written down in a meeting minute, an email, or best of all of course, in a contract.

Positive, but disorganized and often promises too much

The Energetic Guy will rarely make any notes from a phone call or a meeting—and if he does, he will definitely lose them. So you will want to come prepared with documents or summaries that you can hand out during or at the end of a meeting. And after each meeting you should send him a clear email confirming what you talked about, what you agreed, and what the road forward is.

Tie him down there and then

Be organized for him

On the positive side, as long as you remain friendly and positive, you can be quite up front with an Energetic Guy. You can usually ask directly for a favor—they tend to be very forthcoming and helpful. And as I said, when you do get a promise, make sure you make it clear how you understood the promise and what you expect him to do.

You can be upfront and ask for favors

Here I have included just a brief example to illustrate how you can use the keenness of an Energetic Guy to make him promise very clearly something that perhaps goes a bit beyond what he intended.

"I know we haven't worked together for long, but it would really mean a lot to me if you could have a quick look at this project for me and perhaps offer some advice on how we can get going. I am trying to get Diddlydoo Studios on board, and I understand you know Dave who works there, right?"

"Yes, I do... "

"Great! I really appreciate it! So you'll have a word with Dave after you read through it?"

"Um, yeah, sure. I'll read through it for you."

Then after the conversation, send an email thanking him for "reading through the document and talking to Dave about it" and also say that "It would be great if you could let me know what Dave thought of it." If you really want to be pushy, and with an Energetic Guy it usu-

ally pays to be, ask him for a date, for example, "Do you think you'll have a chance to talk to Dave this week?" You will rarely get a "no" from an Energetic Guy. But if you do push it too far, you may find that they suddenly become very difficult to get hold of.

The second personality type I want to discuss is the **Business Guy**. The Business Guy, as the name indicates, is all about business. He makes quick and clear decisions; he is usually very opinionated—and when he's made up his mind, nothing you can do will make him change it again.

The Business personality

Quick to make decisions and stubborn

The Business Guy is very clear on what he likes and what he thinks is possible. But he or she (usually the former) may be very, very difficult to talk to. He will shake his head while you talk, interrupt, and in general feel much more difficult to handle than the Energetic Guy. You need to adapt your way of talking to the way the Business Guy likes to communicate. They do not want to hear about your fishing trip last week; they do not want a 20-minute PowerPoint of the background of your new project. They want to know what you can do for them. Get that right and you may walk out of the meeting with a signed contract in your hand.

Very clear in his communication

Be direct and focused in your communication

How to Become a Celebrity

He may test you

Remember that the Business Guy often behaves in a way intended to test you. He may interrupt you or be extremely dismissive, just to see if you have courage and backbone. But don't get too cocky with him. Stick to a serious business tone in your communication, and make sure you are well prepared even for a short meeting!

The Hesitant personality

The last personality type I want to discuss is the **Hesitant Guy**. Now, the title may not do the personality justice, but it is hard to find a good term for them (some sales books refer to them as "the Precise Customers"). The Hesitant Guy is a sticker for details and needs every little box on the form ticked before he or she (quite often the latter) moves on. You tend to find such personalities in middle management positions, but even highly successful businessmen can have this type of personality. They never make a decision based on gut feelings or because they "just like you." When you communicate with a Hesitant Guy, make sure you don't get overly enthusiastic; talk slowly and in a structured way and above all be well-prepared. (The Hesitant Guy tends to do a lot of research.)

Sticker for details

Often found in middle management positions

Don't get too carried away—talk slowly and always be well prepared

Identify his needs and tick his boxes and you will sell

The good thing about Hesitant Guys is that they can shop with their heads rather than their hearts. When you realize this, it all boils down to a proper needs analysis and then showing that you or your project ticks all the right boxes. Handle the Hesitant Guy this way, and you will find him a very easy partner to work with.

7.3.4 LEARN TO LISTEN

Whether you sell a product, a service, or just yourself, being a good listener is a key to being good at selling. It is also the part of selling that most people seem to struggle the most with.

> A good seller must know how to listen

Why is listening is so important in selling? After all, you have just learned that you can control the call effectively by using questions. Does it really matter what the other guy says if you can still control the conversation? Yes! First of all, people will very quickly realize it if you are not listening well, simply because you ask a question they've already answered earlier in the call or because you make a statement that contradicts information they have provided, or simply because when you don't listen properly your pace and timing doesn't match that of a normal conversation. And if people feel you are not listening, they also feel that you don't care about them or their interests. And who wants to do business with someone who doesn't care? Second, not listening will make you miss buying signals,

> Listening creates trust

> Listen for buying signals and potential objections

things that the person says that you could use to close a sale or an agreement immediately. And third, if you don't listen you won't have any idea what the other person is thinking or—if on the phone—doing. Is he reading the newspaper or checking his email, or is he actually paying attention to you?

> What is the other person doing?

So from this we can deduct that when you are listening to the other part in a sales conversation or a negotiation, what you want to listen for falls into three separate categories: mood, obstacles, and buying signals.

> Listen for mood, obstacles, and buying signals

Understanding the other party's **mood** is vital for your timing and your pitch. When you are in a meeting you can judge someone's mood from how she behaves: is she looking you in the eyes, is she fiddling with her mobile phone? On the phone, however, all you have to go by is her voice. Does she sound interested? Does she answer quickly and with meaningful sentences? If the other person started off answering with full sentences and now is just answering with "aha" and "mm" noises, you can be pretty sure you are losing her.

> Understanding the other party's mood is vital for your timing and your pitch

> Does he answer quickly and with meaningful sentences?

Other indications that you are losing a person's attention—and losing the deal—are keyboard chatter in the background and

> Keyboard chatter

pauses between your questions and the person's answers. (He probably had you on a speaker and was doing something completely different, like eating his lunch or reading his emails.) As soon as you get any indication that you are losing the other person's attention, get it back immediately!

If you think the other person is losing attention—get it back!

The owner of one of the biggest US call centers—who was just another seller (albeit a great seller) when I first met him many years back—told me he always tried to form a mental image of what the person on the other end of the line was doing. Was he listening and taking notes? Was she writing an email to someone else while you talk, or was she making coffee? If you can envision what the other person is doing, you can also prevent problems and get her attention back at the right time.

Form a mental image of what the other person is doing

Listening for **obstacles** is important because you need to know they are there and overcome them before you close a deal. If you call trying to convince a restaurant to book your rock band for a gig, and during the call the other party says something along the lines of "we already have an agreement with a jazz band that plays here regularly" you definitely want to make sure you have given some great arguments for why he or she should try your

Listening for obstacles so you can overcome them before you close a deal

band instead (that you would draw a different crowd, that he can still keep the existing arrangement as you can play on different days, etc). Perhaps not the best illustration, but you do get my drift.

Look at obstacles as a great way of closing

Instead of looking at obstacles as a negative thing—something that can prevent a deal—the best sellers look at obstacles as a great way of closing. Obstacles are often actually the customer saying "I'm interested but," and if you can solve that "but" you will have a deal.

> *An illustration: "I'm sorry, but our bar isn't really set up for live music." This would make most people give up trying to book a gig immediately. The fainthearted would simply go "Oh, I see. Thanks for your time." The true seller understands that this is actually an opportunity to get a deal. "Oh, I see. I'll tell you what I can do. If you really are interested in this, I will call one of my contacts and see if he can supply a mobile scene for free and we would take care of all the other equipment. I am not sure I'll manage, but if I can, what day would be best for you? Tuesday or Thursday?" Suddenly it has become very hard to reply with anything except one of those days. Then all you have to do is to follow*

up with "Great! If I can arrange all the equipment and a scene, I guess we have a deal! Give me an hour or so to check, and I'll get back to you to confirm."

Handling objections well is a key part to good selling. You can find more information on useful techniques to handle objections in chapter 7.3.5.

> Handling objections well is a key part to good selling

Listening for **buying signals** is important because those are the little openings for you to enter the closing phase. Sticking to the above rock band example, if the restaurant owner were to say things like, "We were going to have The Bananas here on Friday, but they canceled," or "We used to have live music every Thursday, but the costs were just too high," you have some obvious openings to enter into the closing part of the call: "I'm sorry to hear that! We're actually booked for Friday, but I could try to juggle things around. If I can make the arrangements, what time would you want us to be there on Friday?" or "Look, I know that some of the high-profile bands have been increasing their charges a lot—including ourselves—but I really think that The Fork is a perfect venue for us. If I can get you a really good price, what date would be the best for you, the 14th or the 15th?" From then on it's all a matter of sticking to

> Buying signals are openings for you to enter the closing phase

the closing. Don't go back to the informative phase. Now you just need the verbal handshake and the deal is done.

Change from product talk to closing when you hear buying signals

As soon as you hear a buying signal, you should change from pitching your product to actually closing the deal. Sadly many people don't—either because they don't hear the buying signals or because they are so focused on their own pitch or product that they are unable to stop talking about what they are selling.

> *A few years back I was coaching a very good, but also very young, voiceover talent, teaching him how to actively sell his services to the advertising industry. We had been writing some pitch scripts for him and had identified some good selling points: his previous experience in radio broadcast, a voice that captured listeners, he had his own studio and could deliver recordings very fast. He had spent some time practicing his pitch and also practicing leading the conversation forward through his pitch by asking questions actively. He now felt ready to start calling. I was listening to the conversation on another line and after not getting past the gatekeepers on his first few calls, he finally got to speak*

to a project manager at a medium-sized advertising agency. About two minutes into the call, this happened:

"Voiceover talent: ...and one of the things I can offer is my own studio and the ability to supply voiceovers according to scripts within days—sometimes even hours. I presume sometimes you have jobs where there are quite short deadlines?

Manager: Well, we do usually plan so as to leave us with comfortable deadlines for all parties, but of course sometimes things come up that we cannot control. Today, for example, the file voiceover for one of our TV advertisements turned out to be corrupt and he is not available to do a new recording this week, so the whole project is being held up...

Voiceover talent: Yes, I see. I am able to supply all types of file formats of course. What file formats do you usually work with?"

At this time I was gesticulating wildly, which obviously threw his attention off. Here was a potential customer literally saying he was stuck—a whole *project delayed—because he couldn't get a voiceover actor to redo a failed recording this week. And the voiceover talent calling to sell himself simply moved on through his own pitch, asking about file formats! Another three minutes into the call, the manager politely agreed to take down his contact details and let him know if something should come up in the future. A voiceover talent called someone who was desperately in need of an urgent voiceover, and because he wasn't listening for buying signals, they couldn't reach an agreement! It sounds absurd, but this happens all the time—both to professional sellers and people like you and me. What the voiceover talent should have done, of course, was to immediately register the buying signal, throw his sales pitch out the window, and go straight for closing:*

"Really? Well it is very fortunate that I called, then! Look, what I'll do, since you're in a bit of a spot, is to run home to my studio, do a few recordings and get them over to you to listen to. Since we haven't worked together before, I'll do it free of charge and you only pay me if you use the recording. Does that sound OK? If you email me the script now, I'll get right on it."

Even if in the end they decided not to use him for this project, it would have gotten recordings over to them that they were guaranteed to listen to—and with the quality of this guy's voiceovers, he would have had regular jobs from this agency within weeks.

Some buying signals are too small for you to go directly to closing. But write them down. These are the little convincers that you will use when you are ready to go for the close.

> Some buying signals are too small for you to go directly to closing but they may still come in handy

7.3.5 HANDLING OBJECTIONS

In every negotiation and in any sales interaction—whether selling yourself or a product—you will sooner or later meet some type of objection. Many people find this a very tricky phase, and it can very easily lead to a confrontation. This is particularly a problem when you identify closely with what you are selling, such as your own acting skills, your band's performance, your own book, etc.

> Many people find handling objections very difficult

The most important aspect of handling objections is to realize that it is a natural phase of any sale. This is simply how things work. If people just wanted your product on their own, if they didn't need any convincing, the world wouldn't need sellers!

> Objections are a natural phase of any sale

Objections relating to you

The first type of objection you are likely to meet is the objection relating to your presence in the first place. "I don't have time right now," or "We are not looking for a new band at this time," and so forth are such objections. These types of objections can be very frustrating because if you don't handle them correctly they will prevent you from even getting to pitch your product. Getting this sort of initial reply on call after call is also extremely demotivating.

Realize that it is not personal

There are three things you need to know in order to handle this sort of immediate rejection. First, realize that it is not personal. This is just how a lot of busy people respond to unknown callers or visitors.

Never, ever argue or disagree when selling

Second, you need to learn the basic rule of objection handling: never ever argue with the other person. If you learn only one sales technique from this book, it should be this one, so I'll say it again. Never, never, never argue with a person to whom you are trying to sell something. If you want to convince someone to buy something from you or enter into a project with you—or even just employ you—arguing in a negative way is never going to get you anywhere. And by arguing I mean any sort of immediate and clear contradiction. Using words or phrases

Avoid any clear contradiction

like "but," "I am not sure if I totally agree with you there," or "that is perhaps not entirely correct" are big no-no's. It doesn't matter what the person says. If he says, "You don't have the experience we are looking for," your immediate reaction will be to say "but…" and give some argument for why this is not correct. Don't! How often have you had an argument with someone and within a few minutes they have said, "You're right! I've been a complete idiot. What you have been saying all along makes sense now." It just doesn't happen. The other person is the key to whatever you want to achieve (a sale, a role, a gig). You don't want him or her to be in a negative mood; you want the conversation always to remain positive. If someone says, "You don't have the experience we are looking for," the right way to respond is to say something to make him feel he was right, but still give an argument to hire you: "I fully understand your concerns; this job is obviously quite unique. I do believe, however, my wide experience from XYZ would prove very valuable for the job. So what would it take, for you to be convinced that I'm the right man for the job? I tell you what, I'll come over to your office and meet you for just a few minutes and I am sure you will see that I am the person you're looking for. Will you be in the office this afternoon?" It may not con-

Avoid "but"

The other person is the key to whatever you want to achieve—don't make him dislike you!

Agree—but still get your point across

vince the other person, but it certainly gives you a better chance than saying, "I think you are wrong about this."

Just a quick question...

This relates somewhat to another technique you really need to know in order to be successful getting your foot in a door, a technique most professional sellers refer to as the "quick question technique." It basically involves agreeing totally with the other party's objection, but then saying that you just need to ask a couple of quick questions:

> "Look, I'm very busy at the moment and we don't discuss new film projects on the phone."

> "I fully understand, Joe. If I could just ask you a couple of quick questions. You guys were the production company behind the nature documentary, Love and War in Borneo, right?"

Engage the other person in a conversation

Get a conversation started

The whole purpose of this strategy is to engage the other person in a conversation. As soon as the conversation starts flowing, you can start pitching. But if you try to pitch your idea or product at this stage, the other person will just hang up or get rather nasty on the phone. So you want to ask questions that might engage the other person enough to get a conversation started, and yet keep it as relevant as possible.

Another type of objection you undoubtedly will encounter comes later in the call, after you've had a chance to run through most of your sales pitch. These objections are usually more specific and more "intelligent," referring to either your product or service or the cost.

As I have mentioned briefly earlier, these objections are good! It means that the other person has some sort of basic interest in what you are offering. He also presents a perfect opportunity to close as soon as you've handled the objection.

> Specific objections are good; this indicates a fundamental interest

Most sellers love objections relating to price. These are very clear and easy to handle. And provided you can meet the other party's request you can close and handle the objection at the same time:

> Use objections on price to tie down the customer immediatel

> "John, I'll be honest with you. I like your band. But the guys playing for us now charge nearly 20% less than you guys. I really don't think we can afford to change to you guys."

> "Look, Peter, I fully understand. I tell you what I'll have a word with my part-

ners to see if we can match what you are paying today. If I can arrange this, would you want us to start next Friday or Friday the 21st?"

With that approach the deal is basically done. It is extremely difficult for a potential contract partner who presented price as the deal breaker to not offer you the gig if you can get him the price he wants. All you have to do is get a positive reply on the start date and then say, "Could you hold the line just a second while I get an approval on the price from my partners? They are sitting in the room with me."

> Realize that the objection is an indication of an interest in your product, and then try to solve the objection and close at the same time

Objections relating to other aspects of your offer can be more complicated because they can relate to aspects that you cannot change as easily or aspects of your service that cannot easily be measured against a competitor (in the example above if you replace price with type of music, for example). But the approach is the same. Realize that the objection is an indication of an interest in your product, and then try to solve the objection and close at the same time.

7.3.6 HOW TO DEAL WITH GATEKEEPERS

> Gatekeepers stand between you and the decision maker

When trying to build a career in the entertainment industry, you will very soon realize that between you and the people who can kick-start your career, stand receptionists, switchboard operators, PAs and secretaries. A group of people who seem hellbent on preventing you from getting through to the people that actually matter. Sellers usually refer to these people as "gatekeepers," although much worse descriptions can be heard in sales offices around the world on bad days.

First of all it is important to understand why the gatekeepers are there in the first place. You can be pretty sure they are not there solely to annoy you—although it may feel like they are—so you need to understand the gatekeeper's role in the company. This is important partly in order to bypass the gatekeeper, partly to work with the gatekeeper when you are unable to bypass him or her, and partly to make sure you don't bypass a gatekeeper that might turn out to be the de facto decision maker.

Make sure you understand the gatekeeper's role in the company

So let's look at the different types of gatekeepers. First you have the **Human Switchboard.** (It sounds degrading, I know, but it is the easiest way of describing them so that you understand what they do.) These are basically people whose job it is to say "Welcome to Dull, Dull, and Dully (...) hang on one moment and I'll put you through." In compa-

The Human Switchboard

nies where the decision maker is receiving a lot of calls, be it from sellers or people trying to get an audition or meeting, they will, however, quite often have been given some basic screening duties. These people have only a few seconds to decide whether they think you are worth the decision maker's time, so getting your opening phrase right is vital.

> These people only have a few seconds to decide. Get your opening phrase right

These Human Switchboards will usually be looking for clues in how you present yourself and how you ask for the decision maker. A trick that often works with larger companies is to make it sound like you've just talked to the decision maker you are trying to reach. "Hi, it's John here again," is often a good start. For a smaller company with a single operator, this may not be a good idea though, for obvious reasons. Some preparation is vital too: never ever ask for a person by his role; ask for a person by his name. So don't say, "Could you put me through to your director of marketing, please?" Say, "Is James Directorson around?" If you seem to know James, it is natural for the operator to presume James knows you too.

> Make it sound like you've just talked to the decision maker

> Prepare!

> Never, ever ask for a person by his role; ask for a person by his name

Many gatekeepers of this type have been instructed to ask you for your reason for calling. Be prepared for this. You do not want to sound insecure or like you are hiding something. I find that a partial disclosure here

> The reason for calling

7: Become a seller

works best, unless of course you do in fact have a very, very good reason for calling. "It's regarding the casting process for XYZ," is better than, "I'm trying to get an audition." Sometimes, you may have sent the decision maker an email beforehand, and then it is usually acceptable to describe it as an ongoing discussion. "It's regarding the new documentary I have been discussing with him," might work quite well in such situations.

A different and perhaps more challenging type of gatekeeper is **The Assistant**. These can be PAs, administrative, or executive assistants. Although their exact role in an organization varies, these have a much closer relationship with the decision maker and won't so easily fall for simple sales tricks. They usually know who their boss has spoken to and what project the boss is involved in. The best strategy is to treat these people as a decision maker in their own right. You basically have to pitch your idea to them first, and get them on board. This will not only make them feel important and respected, but it will also hopefully help gain you important allies. If you do your job right and sell the product, service, or concept to The Assistant, he will often do the actual sales job for you. In many cases, he is in fact the de facto decision maker unless you are talking about some very important project.

> The Assistant: PAs, administrative, or executive assistants
>
> These have a closer relationship with the decision make
>
> Treat these people as decision makers in their own right
>
> Get them to sell the idea for you to the decision maker

As I said, however, the actual importance of The Assistant varies from company to company. It is important to try to find out exactly what influence the person has. If you have sold the idea to The Assistant, but then still get no positive confirmation back that the boss is on board, you need to convince The Assistant to let you talk directly with the decision maker.

> Find out exactly what influence the person has

Another type of gatekeeper is **The Researcher**. Such people usually have a dedicated screening job, and this makes it even more important to treat them as decision makers in their own right. Again you should make a full disclosure of why you are calling or visiting, and you should pitch the idea directly to them as you would pitch it to their boss. Never underestimate the importance and influence of The Researchers! In the vast majority of cases, their recommendation is followed by the decision maker.

> Researchers

> Make a full disclosure and pitch directly as if they are decision makers in their own rights

The final type of gatekeepers I want to discuss is **The Partner**. In many smaller companies a decision maker may just forward his phone to a colleague or business partner when he is out, or a colleague may just answer the phone on the decision maker's desk when she hears the phone ringing. Their actual relationship with and influence over the decision maker

> Business partners

> Actual relationship with the decision maker will vary

will vary hugely. It is therefore often best to just try to establish how or when you can reach the actual decision maker. The best approach is a friendly tone combined with minimum disclosure: "Hi! John here. I was trying to reach Peter?" Again this gives the impression that the caller is a friend of the decision maker and since this person is answering someone else's phone they will most likely not want to insult you. When you have introduced yourself like this, simply ask when Peter will be in. Asking for a mobile number might sometimes work, but the downside is that a lot of people are very restrictive about giving out colleagues' phone numbers—and if you really were a close friend, you'd probably have it already.

> Be careful when asking for mobile numbers

7.3.7 HANDLING VOICEMAIL

Voicemail has become a standard part of every business telephone system. For someone fighting on the career ladder for a place among the few selected celebrities, however, it can be both a blessing and a curse.

Most professional sellers that I know generally try to avoid leaving a voicemail message. The reason is simple: when leaving a voicemail you announce that you have called and basically hand away the control of the future communication, or at least the next step,

> Most sellers try to avoid leaving a voicemail message

Leaving a message may give away the initiative

to the other person. If you leave a message asking for a callback, you need to give the person time to actually call you back. It would be seen as rude leaving such a message, and then again calling yourself 30 minutes later. This can seriously delay progress in closing a deal, and even if you wait for a reasonable amount of time before calling again, you can easily be dismissed with a simple, "Yeah, John, I got your message. I'll call you back as soon as I have had more time to look at this." So the general rule, if you want to keep in control of the progress of the deal, is to simply not leave a message.

Sometimes a message must be left

Sometimes, however, leaving a message is something that cannot be avoided. Either because you have unsuccessfully tried to reach the person many times, or because you for one reason or another need to announce that you have called (for example because you had agreed to call back at a specific time). In those cases you need to use the voicemail as a sales tool—to use that technology to your advantage.

Adapt your message style

When you leave a message on a voicemail, always make sure to adapt your message style to the personality of the person you are calling. If you have already spoken to the person, hopefully you have made a mental note of the type of person you are dealing with (see chapter 7.3.3). Was he an Energetic Guy, a Business Guy, or a Hesitant Guy?

If you are calling for the first time, listen carefully to the voicemail greeting. The Energetic Guy is usually quite easy to recognize, even on a recording of just a few seconds. Typically they will sound upbeat, humorous, and often a bit roundabout in their message. A typical message will sound like "Hi there! You've just reached Peter! I'm obviously doing something very important now, but if you leave your name and phone number, I'll call you right back." If you adapt your message to Peter's upbeat style, you are much more likely to get a call back: "Hi Peter! John here. I've got some great news on the gig we discussed last week and really want to discuss this with you, so give me a call back at 555-6666. That's 555-6666."

Listen carefully to the voicemail greeting

Upbeat style for energetic personalities

The Business Guy, on the other hand, will have a very short message, straight to the point. Often they will even leave their default automated message. These guys either don't have the time, or at least pretend not to have the time, to record long, funny greetings. Leave a message in the same style: "John Doe here. New development regarding the gig. Give me a call as soon as you can at 555 6666. That's 555 6666".

Straight to the point with business personalities

> **Be clear and brief when leaving messages for hesitant personalities**

Finally the Hesitant Guy: He will sound very neutral in his greeting. Such personalities will use standard phrases and usually include their full name: "You've reached Peter Esitant. Leave a message after the tone". Don't leave long messages here. Just make sure to speak slowly and clearly when you leave a message for this type of person: "Hi Peter, it's John here. Just wanted to get back to you regarding some development for the gig. Give me a call at 555-6666. That's 5-5-5-6-6-6-6."

> **Consider sending SMS instead of leaving a voicemail.**

One more thing to consider before you leave a message on a voicemail though: A recent study by Opinion Research found that cell phone users under 30 are four times more likely to respond within minutes to text messages than to voicemail. So if you know the person you are calling is young or at least very techno-friendly, it may be worth not leaving a voice message, but instead sending a text. When you do so, make sure you make the message look professional! That means no fancy shorthand like "AAMOI," "4 U," "2nite," and so on. And no smileys or little fancy symbols. Just a brief text stating why you called and why the person should call back: "Hi Peter. Tried to reach you regarding gig. New development. Call me at 555-6666. John."

8 WORKING WITH AGENTS

8.1 Do you really need an agent?

As we will get back to, finding the right agent can be very, very hard work. And let us be frank—there is nothing an agent can do for your career that you can't do yourself. So, do you really need an agent? Trust me, you do. Because while there may not be anything an agent can do for your career that you can't do yourself, there are few things that you can do for your career that an agent can't do way, way better. If you want to make it to the top, you need a really good agent.

Finding the right agent can be hard—but it is worth it!

An agent (in the entertainment industry often referred to as a talent agent or booking agent) is a person whose job it is to find work for you. Whether you are an actor, an author, a director, a producer, a musician, or a model, your agent will actively look for jobs for you. Of course you can and should continue to look for jobs yourself too, but your agent—if he is any good—will have a huge advantage. Many casting directors or other people in the

Agents actively look for work for you

industry looking for talents will go straight to agencies, preferably agencies they have worked with before, to find the artists they are looking for.

Talent packages

Because agencies, at least the biggest ones, represent a broad range of talents, of whom some are well-known and some are up-and-coming, agencies may also "package" talents together. In some cases this packaging may involve the whole initial phase of a project. Let me try to explain: let's say that Agency XYZ has a script from one of their writer talents that they really see a lot of potential in. But the writer is fairly unknown. So they approach one of their hottest acting talents, someone who has recently had a major role in a box office hit, for example, and ask him if he would be willing to take on the leading role. They may even involve one of their director talents and a few minor acting talents. Now suddenly they don't just have a good script from an unknown writer. They have a good script, a hot actor, a top director and so on. They can now basically approach one of the major studios with a package that is more or less ready, and the script by the unknown writer suddenly starts looking very appealing.

Agents review the breakdowns and submit your details continuously

Still not sure if you really need an agent? Well, remember that an agent works for you, not for the studios. A good agent will spend most of the day on the phones, looking through the "breakdowns" (a daily list of all the acting roles sought by studios and casting directors) and submitting photos and information to directors. They will basically do anything they can in order to get you as many auditions as possible. Since agencies are generally paid a commission on what you make, they have to do this in order to make as much money as possible.

> Agencies usually operate entirely on a commission basis

8.2 How to find the right agent?

OK, this is a tricky one. Let's first talk a little bit about the Hollywood agencies. If you are trying to break through in another industry or in another country, the names may be different but the basic structure will be the same.

In Hollywood you have four big agencies: Creative Artists (CAA), The William Morris Endeavor Agency (WME), International Creative Management (ICM), and United Talent Agency (UTA). These are known as the "Big Four" and represent the A-list of agencies.

> The Big Four

> They used to be the "Big Five" until 2009 when Endeavor and the William Morris Agency merged to form William Morris Endeavor.

Be realistic when looking for an agency	Unless you are reading this book while at the same time starring in a major role in the next big box office hit, you need not waste your time calling any of these agencies. In fact, you never have to waste your time calling these, since they will contact you if they want to work with you.
Be aware of scams	Then you have the B, C, and D levels of agencies. And then you have the X level, which are shady men in offices rented for a week, trying to get you to pay some upfront fees before they take off to Aruba until things cool down.
Theatrical agents, commercial agents, and combined agents	So if you are reading this book, you want to aim for the B, C, and D level agencies. Some agencies focus on theatrical roles, some commercial, and some combine both.
SAG Franchised agent or an ATA/NATR agent	You want to make sure that your agent is either "SAG Franchised" (this basically means they are licensed and registered with The Screen Actors Guild) or an ATA/NATR agent (Association of Talent Agents/National Association of Talent Representative).
Online directories	*On SAG's homepage (http://www.sagaftra.org, look under agency relations), you can search for SAG and ATA/NATR agencies in your area. ATA and NATR also have search functions on their own homepages.*

8: Working with agents

Agents are normally paid a commission of 10%. That's it. If you don't work, they don't make any money. If an agent tries to convince you to pay any upfront fees, it should be a big red flag. The same applies if the agent insists that you pay for new headshots through their own photographer, or if they try to sell you anything: books (present book obviously excluded), classes, and so forth. Your agent may have recommendations for anything from photographers and literature to acting classes, but you would normally arrange and pay those separately, not through the agent.

Standard commission is 10%

Be wary of agencies requesting upfront fees.

> SAG rules generally prohibit any upfront fees and any fee for auditioning for roles. You can read more about this on SAG's homepage (see particularly section 11 of the SAG-AFTRA Rules and Regulations).

SAG rules prohibit any upfront fees and any fee for auditioning for roles

When you have decided on some agencies that may be of interest to you (unless the list is very long, expect to amend it as you work your way through it), it is time for the selling skills that you have learned earlier in this book. Some people say, "Don't call or visit agencies, it's considered rude." I say most people who consider this rude are people still looking for an agent. Having said that, however, you really want to approach a potential agent with due

Use your selling skills to sell yourself actively!

Be respectful

respect. These are busy people and deserve a lot of respect for the job they do. You do not call them 10 times a day; you do not send 10 emails in a week. Most agents have a queue of potential clients; an agent is unlikely to decide to work with you if he hates you. But persistence does not necessarily have to be rude. Persistence is about using sales techniques and interpersonal skills to be liked and yet get what you want.

Persistence does not necessarily have to be rude

The standard first approach to an agent used to be a manila envelope with a cover letter and headshot with an attached résumé. Emails used to be a big no-no. But agencies are moving with the times, at least the ones you want to work with, and today most agencies are happy to accept emails.

Modern communication methods

Your email should be short and concise. It should simply state what you are seeking (that would be "agent representation") and two lines maximum about yourself. The agent isn't going to pay much attention to the email text itself. What the agent is looking for is the attachments. You need to attach some head shots. This is a good place to spend money—the better the headshots, the better the chances of getting accepted. It is amazing what a difference a top quality photographer can make. What headshots you want to select

A top quality photo portfolio can make a huge difference

depends on the agency you are seeking. Commercial and model agencies may be happy with just three or four portrait head shots and a couple of profile shots. Theatrical agencies will need more diverse headshots, at least four or five headshots showing your range and personality. Also attach a short résumé. This résumé needs to be tailored for the specific agent. Don't use the CV you used when applying for a job at the local McDonald's. When you write your résumé, make sure you keep it relevant. The agent is not interested in the fact that you attended Clearwater Kindergarten for two years between 1986 and 1988, and he is not going to be impressed by the fact that you won an award as the "best organized student" in third grade. He may, however, be interested in the fact that you have a PADI diving license and have been doing karate for six years, as it may be relevant for some potential jobs.

| Attach a short résumé |

| Keep it relevant |

Submitting the above, however, is also what everyone else is going to be doing too. Now you need to make sure you stand out a bit. A good show reel is important. Most people who make a show reel will do it with a video camera on a tripod in their living room. That's neither going to land you many jobs nor attract many agents. Here is also a good place to spend some money. Get a professional to help you out with the recording, the cutting,

| Make sure your application stands out |

| A show reel |

and the editing. Also get professional help at reducing the file size without loss of quality. Most agents are not happy receiving an email with a 700MB attachment. Upload the compressed video to an online video hosting site and send only the links.

Build a website

To stand out even more, build a website. And make it look good! You can easily buy readymade website templates on such sites as templatemonster.com. Opt for a clean design that is easy to navigate. You want to make sure that the essential details such as videos, images, list of previous work, etc., are easy to find. Include a link to your website in your signature and on your résumé.

When submitting applications online, make it short and relevant

Some agencies limit the contact information they make available. This is basically an indication that the agency has more potential clients than they can handle and they want to reduce the number of phone calls and emails they receive. In fact, a lot of agencies will just have an online form on their website—no numbers, no emails. When sending online inquiries through such websites it is extremely important to stick to the points. Immediately get to the "Why should you work with me?" Then include direct links to your online photos, online videos, and online résumés. Don't expect them to browse around on your website to find these.

Refer to the previous chapters in this book for more information about how you can make your application stand out. (If you skipped straight to this chapter to save time, you are just fooling yourself.) Remember the power of direct or indirect referrals, for example.

Remember the power of direct or indirect referrals

Most likely you will not get a reply. Don't get discouraged. And definitely don't get desperate and start spamming all the agencies in the country with applications. If you are just starting up in the business, it is OK to contact a few agencies at the same time. But you should tailor each application closely to the agency you are contacting. Don't go bananas and send 200 emails in one evening.

Never ever spam agencies with applications

Allow some time to pass, but if you don't get a reply within 7 to 14 days (and you really do need to be prepared mentally for this to happen), you should follow up with a call. Your call will most likely be answered by a receptionist. You will recognize this as a typical gatekeeper from chapter 7.3.6. You need to use your, by now, well-honed selling skills to get past her and to the person dealing with new talents and then again use your sales skills to sell yourself without being too pushy

Use the sales skills you have learned

with a person who most likely has no idea who you are and wasn't even planning to look at your email for some time yet—if ever. Now you will begin to appreciate why I have continued to stress the importance of learning sales skills and understanding how to make people do what you want them to do.

8.3 The Catch 22 of SAG

SAG membership is extremely important

If you are aiming for an acting career, you will quickly understand how important a SAG membership is. Most major agents will not consider you as a client until you are either a SAG member or at least what is known as "SAG-E," eligible for SAG membership.

You will equally swiftly become familiar with the extremely frustrating catch 22 of the whole SAG thing. In order to get a role, you will usually need an agent. And in order to get an agent, you need to be a SAG member. The problem with that is that the SAG rules state that "Performers are only eligible to join Screen Actors Guild **after** working on a SAG film in a principal role."

Performers are eligible to join SAG only after working on a SAG film in a principal role

In fact it gets even worse: Nearly every movie and television show has to operate within the guidelines of SAG, which means that they can

8: Working with agents

hire only SAG actors for major roles or else they have to pay a hefty fine for casting someone outside the union.

So let's summarize. You need to be a SAG member to get a role. But in order to be a SAG member you need to have had a role.

The catch 22: You need to be a SAG member to get a role. But in order to be a SAG member you need to have had a role...

Sounds frustrating? It is! Ask any actor trying to break into the business and they will explain for hours exactly how frustrating. It will usually involve a lot of swearing, and as the night goes on, perhaps a bit of crying. But never forget that there are a lot of SAG members. So somehow there is a way around this.

This is where you need to be prepared to struggle. You may want to refer back to my motivational texts in chapters 3 and 4 and perhaps have a little peak at chapter 9 at this point. It will take time to become eligible for SAG membership. SAG basically offers two ways to membership. The rules as stated by SAG may sound complicated, but put simply you can become a SAG member either through having worked once as a principal performer on a SAG project—that's a speaking role to you and me—or having worked as an extra for three days at full SAG rates and received three SAG vouchers.

Two principal ways to membership: either through having worked once in a speaking role or having worked as an extra for three days at full SAG rates

SAG vouchers: difficult to get

Now, although obviously easier than getting a principal role (which in general are reserved for SAG members in the first place), getting your three vouchers may not be as easy as it sounds. Not all background work is rewarded with a voucher; only a very limited number of jobs on each production give that benefit.

The rules are a bit complicated, but in general a voucher will be issued for a role that would have been reserved for a SAG member, but for one reason or another was given to a non-member. (The SAG rules regulate how many SAG extras must be hired for each non-SAG member.)

Use your contacts

Some people work as extras for months and months trying to get their three vouchers; others have some contacts and get them within a few days. This is where your contact network will come in handy!

Buying your vouchers: a warning

There are other ways of getting your SAG vouchers. First of all there is a small underground industry selling voucher background work. Buying these is expensive and the business is immoral. Moreover, it is also corruption, and as such represents a criminal activity for both buyer and seller—and if it ever were to come out that you had bought

8: Working with agents

your vouchers it would not be a good thing for your career.

A proper alternative route to SAG membership, though, is membership through a SAG-affiliated union such as AEA, AGMA, ACTRA, and AGVA. If you have been a member of one of these unions for one year and done some union-credited work during that period, you are automatically eligible for SAG membership. Some of the SAG-affiliated unions are considerably easier to join than SAG. AGMA (American Guild of Musical Artists) has, for example, no specific requirements, although joining will obviously be pointless if you do not intend to perform any work in that area.

SAG affiliated unions

It used to be even easier before AFTRA merged with SAG. AFTRA was a completely open union of radio and television artists; you could basically join online and all you had to do to get your SAG membership was to get a paid performance role after joining AFTRA.

AFTRA

How to Become a Celebrity

9 THINGS TO REMEMBER

Do something positive for your career every day. It doesn't have to be something major every day—but do something! Write a short letter to someone to introduce yourself, make a phone call to an agency, take time to write a to-do list for the following week, or simply brainstorm a few more ideas. But do something every day! You will be amazed how far you can get if you take one small step daily.

Remember that things are usually hard for a reason. Take the SAG rules for example. The same rules that make it very difficult for you to get a role as a non-SAG member will eventually protect you and your interests when you finally do become a SAG member yourself.

Have fun! So, you have struggled for years trying to achieve success? All your friends from school are now in good, stable jobs while you share an apartment with five others and sleep on a mattress in a corner? Well, remember that you have two things that your friends don't have: you have freedom and you have a

> Do something positive for your career every day

> Remember that things are usually hard for a reason

> Always remember to have fun!

dream! So make the best out of those two. Not every day has to be a struggle; you are allowed to sleep in and have a bit of fun from time to time (while your "normal" friends get up at 7 A.M. to drive to their boring jobs in a bank).

Find your own mantra or slogan. It doesn't have to be complicated, just something to repeat to yourself when you're having a bad day. Aristotle ones said, "We are what we repeatedly do; excellence is a habit." By acting like you want to become, you can make sure you slowly become what you want. And having a little slogan or mantra to repeat to yourself is a great way to stay on track!

Do less, better! Don't do everything—do less better! Make sure everything you do, counts. Don't try to be good at everything at once; don't try to achieve every goal at the same time. Focus on one thing at a time and make sure you do it really well!

Know your own weaknesses! By knowing your own weaknesses you can spot a problem early and nip it in the bud. Whether it is a tendency to laziness, a tendency to be depressed, a problem in your acting skills—it doesn't matter. If you are aware of it, you can deal with it.

9: Things to remember

Keep track of your goals and your progress. Only if you know exactly what you want to achieve long-term and short-term will you ever have a chance of achieving it. Success isn't a lottery; it's hard work!

Being defeated is only a temporary condition; giving up is what makes it permanent. Whatever crap may happen in your life, if you struggle on, you still have a chance of achieving your goals.

Most people regret what they didn't much more than what they did. Or as Montaigne once said, "My life has been filled with terrible misfortune; most of which never happened." So overcome your fears. You will regret far more not going to that audition or not calling that agent again than you will regret having tried and failed.

Every failure is a lesson in how not to do something. After enough lessons, you will know how to do it. The best way to never learn is to never try.

Keep on going and the chances are you will stumble across something, perhaps when you are least expecting it. No one ever stumbled across something sitting down.

Keep track of your goals and your progress

Being defeated is only temporary; giving up is permanent

You will regret what you didn't do more than what you did

Every failure is a lesson

No one ever stumbled across something sitting down

How to Become a Celebrity

You need extraordinary determination

Successful people are just ordinary people with extraordinary determination.

Losers visualize the penalties of failure. Winners visualize the rewards of success.

Winners visualize the rewards of success

Do something small and positive early in the day, just to get yourself going

Do something small and positive early in the day, just to get a flow started. Simply clean your desk or clean up your inbox. Or wash the dishes, just to get you started. When you have finished that small task you'll feel more positive and ready to go do the next thing. The hardest thing is always to get started and if you can't find the motivation to tackle the big things right away, just do something small to get motivated. Then work your way up.

You will never get another shot at today

And finally, remember that today is gone tomorrow. Tomorrow may be another day, but you will never get another shot at today. Margaret Thatcher once said, "Look at a day when you are supremely satisfied at the end. It's not a day when you lounge around doing nothing; it's when you've had everything to do, and you've done." So make sure you make today count!

APPENDIX

Actors' and performers' unions

1. SAG-AFTRA

SAG-AFTRA represents more than 165,000 actors, announcers, broadcasters, journalists, dancers, DJs, news writers, news editors, program hosts, puppeteers, recording artists, singers, stunt performers, voiceover artists, and other media professionals.

5757 Wilshire Blvd., 7th Floor
Los Angeles, CA 90036-3600
Phone: +1 (855) 724-238
Web: www.sagaftra.org

2. Actors' Equity Association

Actors' Equity Association ("AEA" or "Equity"), founded in 1913, is the labor union that represents more than 49,000 Actors and Stage Managers in the United States. Equity seeks to advance, promote, and foster the art of live theatre as an essential component of our society. Equity negotiates wages and working conditions and provides a wide range of benefits, including health and pension plans, for its members. Actors' Equity is a member of the AFL-CIO and is affiliated with FIA, an international organization of performing arts unions.

165 West 46th Street
New York, NY 10036
Phone: +1 (212) 869-8530
Web: www.actorsequity.org

3. American Guild of Musical Artists

A labor organization that represents the men and women who create America's operatic, choral, and dance heritage.

430 Broadway, 14th Floor
New York, NY 10018
Phone: +1 (212) 265-3687
Web: www. musicalartists.org

4. GIAA: Guild of Italian American Actors

GIAA encourages and promotes positive images of Italian Americans in the mass media and popular culture. GIAA is the only ethnic acting union in the United States. Membership is eclectic, with people from many ethnic groups working together with its historic Italian-American base. GIAA supports a broad range of arts groups that are working to preserve their cultural heritage.

Canal Street Station
P.O. Box 123
New York, NY 10013-0123
Phone: +1 (201) 344-3411
Web: http://giaa.us

5. American Guild of Variety Artists

American Guild of Variety Artists (AGVA) is an American entertainment union representing performers in variety entertainment, including circuses, Las Vegas showrooms and cabarets, comedy showcases, dance revues, magic shows, theme park shows, and arena and auditorium extravaganzas.

363 Seventh Avenue, 17th Floor
New York, NY 10001-3904
Phone: +1 (212) 675-1003
Web: www.agvausa.com

6. Filmmakers Alliance (FA)

Filmmakers Alliance (FA) is a community of film artists bound by a commitment to realize the full creative potential of independent film.

12228 Venice Blvd., Ste. 406
Los Angeles, CA 90066
Phone: +1 (310) 568-0633
Web: www.filmmakersalliance.org

7. Associated Actors and Artistes of America

Associated Actors and Artistes of America (AAAA) is the primary association of performers' unions in the United States. This federation is also referred to as 4As. It is headed by a president. The organization is a member of the American Federation of Labor and Congress of Industrial Organization (AFL-CIO). The individual unions constituting AAAA are not members of AFL-CIO. But in AFL-CIO elections the votes are split based on the interests of member unions.

165 W. 46 St.
New York, NY 10036-2501
Phone: +1 (212) 869-8530
Web: none

8. Hispanic Organization of Latin Actors (HOLA)

In expanding job opportunities for Hispanic actors, HOLA strengthens and supports the available talent pool through its professional educational services and awards for excellence in theatre. Ultimately, HOLA strives for an accurate, informed, and non-stereotyped portrayal of Hispanic culture, people, and heritage in theatre, film, television, radio, and commercials.

107 Suffolk St., Ste. 302
New York, NY 10002
Phone: +1 (212) 253-1015
Web: www.hellohola.org

9. International Alliance of Theatrical Stage Employees (IATSE)

Union representing technicians, artisans, and craftpersons in the entertainment industry including live theatre, film and television production, and trade shows.

10045 Riverside Dr.
Toluca Lake, CA 91602
Phone: +1 (818) 980-3499
Web: www.iatse-intl.org

10. New York Women in Film & Television

New York Women in Film & Television supports women calling the shots in film, television, and digital media. NYWIFT energizes the careers of women in entertainment by illuminating their achievements, providing training and professional development, and advocating for equity. The preeminent entertainment industry association for women in New York, NYWIFT brings together nearly 2,000 women and men working both above and below the line. NYWIFT is part of a network of 40 women in film chapters worldwide, representing more than 10,000 members.

6 East 39th Street, Suite 1200
New York, NY 10016-0112
Phone: +1 (212) 679-0870
Web: www.nywift.org

11. Women In Film Los Angeles

Women In Film increases the visibility of our members and recognizes their achievements through a variety of fund-raising events, including our two signature events, the Crystal + Lucy Awards and The Entertainment Forum.

6100 Wilshire Blvd., Suite 710
Los Angeles, CA 90048
Phone: +1 (323) 935-2211
Web: www.wif.org

12. National Association of Black Actors & Supporters (NABAS)

NABA is a unique organization whose mission is to be an advocate for the Black actor.

110 East 59th Street,
New York, NY 10022
Phone: +1 (212) 252-5160
Web: www.nabas-usa.org

13. National Association of Independent Artists

The mission of the National Association of Independent Artists is to strengthen, improve, and promote the artistic, professional, and economic success of artists who exhibit in art shows.

1426 Hazen, SE
Grand Rapids, MI 49507-3713
Phone: +1 (502) 228-4639
Web: www.naia-artists.org

14. The Actors Fund

The Actors Fund, a nonprofit human services organization founded in 1882, serves all professionals— and not just actors—in film, theatre, television, music, opera, and dance through programs that address their unique and essential needs. A national organization with offices in New York, Los Angeles, and Chicago, The Fund directly serves more than 12,800 performing arts and entertainment professionals across the country every year, and hundreds of thousands through our online resources.

729 Seventh Avenue, 10th floor
New York, NY 10019
Phone: +1 (212) 221-7300
Web: www.actorsfund.org

15. Canadian Actors' Equity Association

Canadian Actors' Equity Association represents professional artists including performers (actors, singers, and dancers), directors, choreographers, fight directors, and stage managers, engaged in theatre, opera, and dance in English Canada.

44 Victoria Street, 12th Floor
Toronto, ON M5C 3C4
Phone: +1 (416) 867-9165
Web: www.caea.com

16. Alliance of Canadian Cinema, Television and Radio Artists (ACTRA)

ACTRA (Alliance of Canadian Cinema, Television, and Radio Artists) is the union of more than 22,000 professional performers working in English-language recorded media in Canada including TV, film, radio, and digital media.

625 Church Street, 3rd floor
Toronto, Ontario M4Y 2G1
Phone: +1 (416) 489-1311
Web: www.actra.ca

17. The North American Actors Association

The North American Actors Association is a network serving the entertainment industry by supporting North American actors with a base in Britain. All members are professional actors who can work on both sides of the Atlantic without restriction, are full members in "good standing" of at least one entertainment union and have proof of professional contracts.

Phone: 07873 371891
Web: http://new.naaa.org.uk

18. Equity

Equity is the UK trade union for professional performers and creative practitioners. As a leading industry organization, Equity is known and respected nationally and internationally for the work they do with, and on behalf of, our members working across all areas of the entertainment industry.

Guild House, Upper St Martin's Lane
London WC2H 9EG
Phone: +44 (0)20 7379 6000
Web: http://www.equity.org.uk

19. The Actors' Guild

The Actors' Guild was founded by a community of professional actors who believed there was a better way to do things. They wanted an organization that brought together key industry professionals, strict joining criteria, and a low membership fee, a center for professionals. The need was so great that the guild has grown very quickly and is now the largest membership organization for ongoing training in the UK. Our website, which is solely geared toward professional actors, gets an average of over 27,000 hits every day.

7 Leicester Place
London WC2H 7RJ
Phone: +44 (0)20 7112 8458
Web: www.actorsguild.co.uk

20. British Equity Collecting Society (BECS)

British Equity Collecting Society (BECS) is the UK's only collective management organization for audio-visual performers. It represents the interests of over 27,000 members in the negotiation and administration of performers' remuneration throughout the European Union territories. BECS also administers artist payments on behalf of Equity and broadcasting companies.

Guild House, Upper St Martin's Lane
London WC2H 9EG
Phone: +44 (0)20 7670 0350
Web: www.equitycollecting.org.uk

21. Musicians' Union

The Musicians' Union is a globally-respected organization which represents over 30,000 musicians working in all sectors of the music business.

60-62 Clapham Road
London SW9 0JJ
Phone: +44 (0)20 7582 5566
Web: www.musiciansunion.org.uk

Talent agents

1. ABRAMS ARTISTS AGENCY (NY)

Since 1977, Abrams Artists Agency has enjoyed a reputation as one of the nation's most respected and diversified talent and literary agencies. With principal offices in New York City and Los Angeles, Abrams represent clients in most areas of the entertainment industry including motion pictures, television, animation, theatre, radio and television commercials, hosting and broadcasting, and all forms of narration.

275 7th Ave., 26th Fl.
New York, NY 10001
Phone: +1 (646) 486-4600
Web: www.abramsartists.com

2. Agency for the Performing Arts (APA)

An industry leader in the field of talent and literary representation for nearly fifty years, APA represents many of today's most talented artists in all areas of the entertainment industry, with principal offices in Beverly Hills, New York, and Nashville. Unique in the industry, APA believes that there should be no delineation between Film, Television, and Theatre. Our artists, including Academy Award, Tony Award, and Emmy Award winning talent, are able to move from features to television series to Broadway at any given moment.

405 S. Beverly Dr.
Beverly Hills, CA 90212
Phone: +1 (310) 888-4200
Web: www.apa-agency.com

3. Alvarado Rey Agency

Originally created in 1941, the Alvarado Rey Agency continues its long tradition of representing talented actors from Latin America, Europe, and the United States theatrically and commercially in Los Angeles.

7906 Santa Mónica Blvd., Suite 205
West Hollywood, CA 90046
Phone: +1 (323) 656-2277
Web: www.alvaradorey.com

4. Angel City Talent

Angel City Talent has solidified itself as a fierce competitor within the entertainment industry. Angel City focuses on maintaining a solid, reliable, and innovative roster of motion picture, television, commercial, print, and hosting talent. Our mission is to enjoy a great collaboration with talent and industry professionals, providing outstanding talent and service with an easy-to-work-with attitude.

8318 Kirkwood Drive
Los Angeles, CA 90046
Phone: +1 (323) 656-5489
Web: www.angelcitytalent.biz

5. Avalon Artists Group

Avalon Artists Group is a bi-coastal, full-service agency founded by Craig Holzberg, a former actor/model who started his career over 25 years ago in Los Angeles. Craig switched gears to work behind the scenes. At Avalon Artists Group, Craig prides himself in being directly involved in all aspects of his clients' careers. Avalon Artists Group is a full-service talent agency representing actors and models of all ages for film, TV, theatre, commercials, voiceover, and print

5455 Wilshire Boulevard, Suite 900
Los Angeles, CA 90036
Phone: +1 (323) 692-1700
Web: www.avalonartists.com

6. Clear Talent Group

Clear Talent Group is a full-service talent agency headquartered in Los Angeles with additional offices in New York and New Orleans with partnerships in Chicago and Atlanta. Established in 2003, CTG has assembled a staff of respected agents that represent actors, models, young people, directors, dancers, choreographers, and designers in all areas of the entertainment industry.

10950 Ventura Boulevard
Studio City, CA 91604
Phone: +1 (818) 509-0121
Web: http://cleartalentgroup.com

7. Creative Artists Agency (CAA)

Creative Artists Agency (CAA) is a prominent entertainment and sports agency headquartered in Los Angeles. It is well-known as Hollywood's leading talent agency and it has numerous famous entertainment-industry clients. Although its main headquarters are in Los Angeles, CAA also has offices in New York City, Chicago, and Nashville, as well as London, Beijing, Dubai, and Stockholm.

2000 Avenue of the Stars
Los Angeles, CA 90067
Phone: +1 (424) 288-2000
Web: www.caa.com

8. Don Buchwald & Associates, Inc. (DBA)

Don Buchwald & Associates, Inc. is a full service talent agency. Our Commercial and Broadcast Departments in New York were the original cornerstones of the business, and continue to be recognized as highly influential in the marketplace. Today they proudly offer representation in all areas of the entertainment industry including our Film, Theatre, and Television department, our Literary department, our Television and Film Packaging departments, our Personal Appearances department, our Syndication Arm (for radio, television and the Internet), and our Youth department in New York, along with a unique joint venture in Los Angeles, the Buchwald Talent Group, which represents youth in all areas.

10 East 44th Street
New York, NY, 10017
Phone: +1 (212) 867-1200
Web: www.buchwald.com

9. ICM Partners

ICM Partners is one of the world's largest talent and literary agencies, with offices in New York, Los Angeles, and London. The agency represents creative and technical talent in the fields of motion picture, television, books, music, live performance, branded entertainment, and new media. ICM Partners was formed in 1975 through the merger of Creative Management Associates and International Famous Agency.

10250 Constellation Boulevard
Los Angeles, CA 90067
Phone: +1 (310) 550-4000
Web: www.icmtalent.com

10. The Gersh Agency

The Gersh Agency, dubbed Gersh or simply TGA, is the only mega-successful family-run agency. They fast-forward young actors' careers, while also taking care of the older clients that are in it for the long haul.

9465 Wilshire Blvd, 6th Floor
Beverly Hills, CA 90212
Phone: +1 (310) 274-6611
Web: www.gershagency.com

11. International Creative Management, Inc. (ICM)

ICM Partners is one of the world's largest talent and literary agencies with offices in New York, Los Angeles, and London. The agency represents creative and technical talent in the fields of motion picture, television, books, music, live performance, branded entertainment, and new media.

10250 Constellation Boulevard
Los Angeles, CA 90067
Phone: +1 (310) 550-4000
Web: www.icmtalent.com

12. Osbrink Agency

This is a tight-knit, smaller agency that specializes in child actors. It was created by a former stage mom, Cindy Osbrink. Today it represents the most bankable tweens, who appear in a range of projects, from controversial Sundance films to hit TV series. Since the inception of The Osbrink Agency over two decades ago, the company has grown into a prestigious full-service agency, providing the Entertainment and Fashion Industry with many of the most visible clients in film, television, commercials, voiceovers and print.

4343 Lankershim Blvd
North Hollywood, CA 91602
Phone: +1 (818) 760-2488
Web: www.osbrinkagency.com

13. Paradigm Talent Agency

Since its founding in 1992, Paradigm has established itself as a leading entertainment talent agency, guiding the careers of an elite roster of actors, musical artists, directors, writers, and producers. Paradigm's select, yet diverse client list allows it to effectively compete with other large agencies while guaranteeing personalized attention to every client. With offices in Los Angeles, New York City, Monterey, California and Nashville, Tennessee, Paradigm provides representation to clients across its motion picture, television, music, comedy and personal appearances, theatre, books, new media, commercial, and physical production departments.

360 North Crescent Drive, North Building
Beverly Hills, CA 90210
Phone: +1 (310) 288-8000
Web: www.paradigmagency.com

14. United Talent Agency (UTA)

Though relatively young, United Talent Agency is part of the "Big Four" Hollywood agencies, along with Creative Artists Agency, WME Entertainment, and International Creative Management. UTA's Production Department was started in 1994 and represents producers, directors of photography, production designers, costume designers, editors, visual effects supervisors, first assistant directors, second unit directors and stunt coordinators. Acting clients like Seth Rogen, Johnny Depp, Ben Stiller, and Jennifer Lopez, are usually the ones getting all the press.

9336 Civic Center Drive
Beverly Hills, CA 90210
Phone: +1 (310) 273-6700
Web: www.unitedtalent.com

15. WME Entertainment

In 2009 Endeavor announced its merger with the William Morris Agency, thus creating the largest talent agency in the world, now known as WME Entertainment. Some of Endeavor's A-List clients have included Dustin Hoffman, Adam Sandler, Ben Affleck, Matt Damon, Jennifer Garner, Keira Knightley, and Tina Fey, among others. By 2008, Endeavor grew to become one of the largest talent agencies in the country, boasting nearly 5,000 employees and representing everyone from actors and writers, to directors and producers.

9601 Wilshire Blvd., 3rd Fl.
Beverly Hills, CA 90212
Phone: +1 (310) 285-9000
Web: www.wmeentertainment.com

16. TalentWorks

TalentWorks was started in 1982 by Harry Gold with only two employees. Within six months, Gold had expanded the agency by adding two of the top children's agents, Ruth Hansen and Joy Stevenson. Over the years, the company has had the honor of representing some of the finest talent in the business: Oscar, Emmy, and Golden Globe winners, as well as many others.

3500 West Olive Ave., Suite 1400
Burbank, CA 91505
Phone: +1 (818) 972-4300
Web: www.talentworks.us

17. Synergy Talent

Established in 2006, Synergy Talent has already made its mark on the entertainment industry, representing talent in Television, Film, Commercials, and Voiceover. Our clients have appeared in Oscar-winning feature films, on Broadway, as series regulars on award-winning television shows and web series, in major national commercial and voiceover campaigns, and on virtually every major television series on the air today.

13251 Ventura Blvd., Suite 2
Studio City, CA 91604
Phone: +1 (818) 995-6500
Web: www.synergytalent.net

18. Stars, The Agency

Stars, The Agency, now celebrating over twenty-five years in business, is a full-service talent agency located in the heart of downtown San Francisco. Stars, which has consistently enjoyed the reputation as one of the largest, most successful and respected agencies on the West Coast, provides a comprehensive list of services, representing men, women, and children for on-camera, voiceover and theatrical work.

23 Grant Avenue, 4th Floor
San Francisco, CA 94108
Phone: +1 (415) 421-6272
Web: www.starsagency.com

19. Independent Talent Group

Independent Talent Group began as a modeling agency and quickly expanded to include actors, writers, directors, and producers. The agency provides the best-connected representation throughout Europe for the arts, but their exclusive status demands fairly impressive credentials to qualify. Celebrity clients include hundreds of influential actors, directors, and media darlings, such as Orlando Bloom, Steven Elder, Rachel Weisz, Thandie Newton, Daniel Craig, and Jonathan Glazer.

Oxford House, 76 Oxford Street
London W1D 1BS
Phone: +44 (0)20 7636 6565
Web: www.independenttalent.com

20. William Morris

The William Morris Agency certainly ranks as one of the most popular acting agencies in London, and the company represents all areas of entertainment, including voiceovers, film, television, publishing, commercials, and theatre. The organization has global reach and can find clients work internationally. A-list stars and celebrities use the company's experienced agents and industry expertise to advance their careers. Current celebrity clients include Hugh Jackman, Steve Martin, the Rolling Stones, Queen Latifah, Kanye West, and Chad Lowe.

Centre Point, 103 New Oxford Street
London WC1A 1DD
Phone: +44 (0)20 7534 6800
Web: www.wma.com

21. Conway Van Gelder

Located in the heart of Soho, Conway Van Gelder offers substantial representation for radio, theatre, film, and television actors. Celebrity clients include Tom Riley, Aisling Loftus, Lee Ingleby, and Jack O'Connell. A strong international presence affords worldwide opportunities.

Third floor 8/12 Broadwick Street
London W1F 8HW
Phone: +44 (0)20 7287 0077
Web: www.conwayvangeldergrant.com

22. Ken McCreddie

Ken McCreddie provides international links for career advancement and offers suitable representation for actors and directors in voiceovers, film, theatre, and other industry areas. A convenient voiceover search tool provides convenient online searches for suitable projects. Celebrity clients include Emily Blunt, Joseph Fiennes, Anna Friel, Anthony Howell, Idris Elba, Tim Curry, Jeremy Irons, Neve Campbell, Helen Mirren, and the late Sir Nigel Hawthorne.

101 Finsbury Pavement
London EC2A 1RS
Phone: +44 (0)20 7439 1456
Web: www.kenmcreddie.com

23. United Agents

United Agents ranks as one of Europe's leading talent agencies for actors, authors, composers, designers, playwrights, and other entertainment professionals. The agency offers competent representation for established and emerging artists. Celebrity clients include Kate Winslet, Alan Bennett, Dawn French, Ricky Gervais, Ewan McGregor, Sienna Miller, Tom Stoppard, Keira Knightley, and Julian Barnes.

12-26 Lexington Street
London W1F OLE
Phone: +44 (0)20 3214 0800
Web: http://unitedagents.co.uk

24. Artist Rights Group

Artist Rights Group has distinguished itself by providing superior contract terms for clients. The agency's focus concentrates on locating quality work that allows actors creative growth and career development. Clients include Anton Du Beke, Dr. Linda Papadopoulos, Karen Williams, Daniel Radcliffe, Justin Bieber, Emma Watson, Tom Felton, Robert Jarvis, Devon Murray, Josh Herdman, and Charles Hughes.

4 Great Portland Street
London W1W 8PA
Phone: +44 (0)20 7436 6400
Web: www.argtalent.com

Acting and voice coaches

1. Larry Moss

Larry has been an acting coach for over 35 years and now is one of the most sought-after acting coaches of our time. He has worked with many of our top stars including Helen Hunt, Hilary Swank, Leonardo DiCaprio, Tobey Maguire, Jim Carrey, Jennifer Garner, David Duchovny, and Tea Leoni.

LMS Studio, Inc
323 West Grand Avenue
El Segundo, CA 90245
Phone: +1 (310) 822-3236
Web: www.larrymoss.org

2. Bob Krakower

Bob Krakower is recognized as one of the top acting teachers and coaches in the business. His clients have been nominated for the Academy Award, the Emmy Award, and the Tony Award. Sought-after by studios, networks, theatre companies, and actors, he works out of home bases in New York and Los Angeles. His studio in New York, housed at One-On-One Productions in NYC, is one of the most successful long-running acting classes in New York.

34 West 27th Street, 11th Floor
New York, NY 10001
Phone: +1 (212) 691-6000
Web: www.bobkrakower.com

3. Stan Kirsch

A native New Yorker and cum laude graduate of Duke University, Stan spent his twenties working successfully as an actor. For the past decade Stan has also been one of the most prominent and sought-after acting coaches in Los Angeles. In that time he has worked with thousands of actors to hone their craft and garner success in an otherwise elusive industry. His clientele, comprised of working actors throughout the business, have booked literally hundreds of roles from TV series regulars to film leads, recurring roles, and guest stars. In 2008 he and his wife formed Stan Kirsch Studios, where he currently works to further the success of actors on a daily basis.

6671 Sunset Blvd. Ste 1584-A
Los Angeles, CA 90028
Phone: +1 (323) 512-1049
Web: http://stankirschstudios.com

4. Jason Bennett

Jason Bennett teaches all the professional level and basic acting classes. The other faculty members teach voice, improvisation, sensory process, movement, and archetype work—often alongside Jason Bennett. Jason Bennett offers a New York Acting School for absolute beginners, non-professionals AND seasoned, award-winning communicators, actors and singers in film, television, theatre, and communications. Jason Bennett was runner-up for Best Acting Coach in NYC, 2010 AND 2011, and runner-up in 2011 for Best Scene Study Teacher, by vote of the readers of the highly prestigious "Backstage!"

520 E 12th St,
New York,
NY 10009
Phone: +1 (917) 494-0068
Web: www.jbactors.com

5. JoAnna Beckson

Along with being a consultant for Disney and Paramount Studios, JoAnna has maintained the dual career of Actress/Director and Teacher of acting in New York City for many years. JoAnna's involvement in the daily "business" of acting gives her special insight toward helping actors develop their craft and solve the problem of finding work. For the past twelve years, JoAnna has also been an Adjunct Professor at New York University's School of Continuing and Professional Studies as well as the Graduate Film Department at NYU Tisch School of the Arts.

242 West 36th Street - 3rd Floor
New York, NY 10018
Phone: +1 (917) 749-6922
Web: www.joannabeckson.com

6. Tisch School of the Arts

For over 45 years, the Tisch School of the Arts has drawn on the vast resources of New York City and New York University to create an extraordinary training ground for artists, scholars of the arts, and creative entrepreneurs. Students who attend New York University's Tisch School of the Arts train in prime territory for the theatre arts in the heart of one of the nation's leading performance cities, New York. Programs use state-of-the-art facilities to train students in television and film. Graduates include Oliver Stone, Alec Baldwin, Spike Lee, and Brett Morgen.

New York University, Tisch School of the Arts
Office of the Dean
721 Broadway, 12th Floor
New York, NY 10003
Phone: +1 (212) 998-1800
Web: http://about.tisch.nyu.edu

7. David Kagen's School of Film Acting

David Kagen's School of Film Acting in North Hollywood, LA, provides professional on-camera acting classes taught by working film and television actors in Los Angeles. Learn from our highly experienced and influential instructors and award-winning actors and writers. David Kagen is a Carnegie-Mellon graduate who has taught and coached successful actors such as Ted Danson, Alec Baldwin, Robin Wright, Giancarlo Esposito, Stacy Edwards, and Ally Walker for almost thirty years. David Kagen works at the top level of the industry.

4854 Laurel Canyon Blvd, Studio Village
Hollywood, CA 91607
Phone: +1 (818) 752-9678
Web: www.davidkagen.com

8. Howard Fine Acting Studio

Howard Fine Acting Studio, one of the most highly respected actor training centers in the world. Since its inception, our outstanding faculty has trained many luminaries of the acting profession. Teaching and nurturing actors in the heart of Hollywood since 1985 and headed by world-renowned acting coach Howard Fine, author of "Fine On Acting: A Vision of the Craft," the studio offer classes for adults, from beginner through to working professionals.

1445 North Las Palmas Avenue
Los Angeles, CA 90028-7720
Phone: +1 (323) 962-3188
Web: www.howardfine.com

9. Alan Dysert

The Actor's School offers classes and workshops with Alan Dysert and other respected instructors from many professions including film, music, and other entertainment industries. Alan trains actors and performers in many cities including Chicago, Miami, Atlanta, Nashville, Memphis, Indianapolis, and others. In Nashville, he has made notable contributions as the acting coach to country music stars. He prepares recording artists for their music videos and consults their record companies on television projects and performance development. In this workshop, Alan focuses on the realities of acting in front of a camera, whether it is for a film, a soap opera, a situation comedy, a commercial, or a music video.

1227 Lakeview Drive 2
Franklin, TN 37067
Phone: +1 (615) 500-7661
Web: www.actorsschoolusa.com

10. Michelle Danner Los Angeles Acting School

The school offers a wide array of classes and workshops that are geared for actors of all ages and levels. Actors are encouraged to raise the bar and work to their full potential. Our mission is to provide a creative home to a community of passionate actors. Our actors are able to master the fundamentals and develop their craft by working on diverse material, honing their skills both on-camera and on-stage.

2437 Main St.
Santa Monica, CA 90405
Phone: +1 (310) 392-0815
Web: www.michelledanner.com

11. The Michael Chekhov Acting Studio

This course is a psycho-physical approach to acting based on the artistic principles left to us by Michael Chekhov as well as other innovators of 20th-century theatre. The technique was developed as a way to apply common and archetypal human conditions to the individuality of the actor. The work is imaginative rather than personal, physical rather than intellectual. The studio will work with impulse and energy, transformation and creation.

138 W 15th St, 1st Floor
New York, NY 10011
Phone: +1 (646) 385-2876
Web: www.michaelchekhovactingstudio.com

12. Bruce Ducat

Ducat has served as the Acting/Dialogue Coach on several television series and pilots from the big three networks, numerous movies for television, and feature films. His long list of coaching clients and acting students, both past and present, includes the stars of feature films, television series, new media, and on and off-Broadway stage productions. His adult list includes Julie Andrews, Jayne Meadows, Jennie Garth, Colleen Camp, Laura Kightlinger, Wil Shriner, and the late Eugene Roche and Chris Farley.

P.O. Box 2264
Toluca Lake, CA 91610
Phone: +1 (818) 332-5777
Web: www.studioactreel.com

13. The Juilliard School

The Juilliard School continues to cultivate talent in students to develop them into passionate, skilled actors and actresses by placing them in front of live audiences through its Professional Intern Program. Students are provided with hands-on experiences in costume, electrics, creating props, painting scenes, stage management, production management, and makeup. Alumni attend regularly to work with students in developing career paths.

60 Lincoln Center Plaza
New York, NY 10023-6588
Phone: +1 (212) 799-5000
Web: http://juilliard.edu

14. Acting School for Film and Television

Created by writer, producer, and actor, Mark Stolzenberg, this school offers one-on-one coaching, special events and classes for acting in television, film and commercials. Improv and comedy classes are also offered. Distinguished alumni have had stand-up shows, have been seen on television shows like "Law and Order" or "Blues Clues," have produced films and written books. Check out the classes offered to find one that caters to your personal interests.

131 W 72nd St, Studio 1
New York, NY 10023
Phone: +1 (212) 877-2219
Web: http://actingclassforfilm.com

15. The Barrow Group

The Barrow Group encourages students to become playwrights, actors, storytellers, teachers, and artists. The organization provides not only acting classes but also offers an arts center, theatre company, and showcases. Classes are provided for both adults and children throughout the year.

312 W 36th St., 3rd Floor
New York, NY 10018
Phone: +1 (212) 760-2615
Web: http://barrowgroup.org

16. Alliance Theatre Acting Program

Celebrating over 30 years of excellence, the Alliance Theatre Acting Program has developed a comprehensive curriculum in stage, film, and television acting. One of the most successful and respected programs in the country, the Acting Program offers students of all ages, experience, and abilities a chance to work with professional theatre and film educators in one of America's most renowned regional theatres.

1280 Peachtree Street NE
Atlanta, GA 30309
Phone: +1 (404) 733-4650
Web: http://alliancetheatre.org

17. Voice Acting Academy

Classroom and tele-course offerings for many aspects of voice acting and perfecting the art of voiceovers, this academy has courses running from shout workshops to six- or eight-week long programs.

13639 Freeport Rd.
San Diego, CA 92129-3210
Phone: +1 (858) 484-0220
Web: www.voiceacting.com

18. Anthony Reece Character Voices

Located in Fort Collins, Colorado, this school offers voiceover training through a variety of programs and workshops, including some for children and private lessons.

P.O. Box 272441
Fort Collins, CO 80527
Phone: +1 (970) 223-3659
Web: www.anthonyreece.com

19. Jon Campbell Acting Classes

Jon Campbell has been in the entertainment industry for over 30 years. They offer teaching in group workshops, 1-to-1, and drama school.

36 Fentiman Road
London SW8 1LF United Kingdom
Phone: +44 (0)78 5469 7971
Web: www.joncampbellacting.co.uk

20. Jude Alderson

Jude coaches privately and in small groups in Camden, London. Her experience as actor, director, and writer in both theatre and film spans 35 years in the profession. She has developed a distinctive approach to acting training that releases and strengthens the actor. Her method has a high success rate in the industry. Jude has worked in close collaboration with casting directors and has many close contacts within the industry, as well as directing and coaching at most of the major London drama and music schools.

Phone: +44 (0) 207 586 8239
Web: http://judealdersonactingcoach.com

21. Dee Cannon

Dee Cannon is one of the most sought-after acting/dialogue coaches in the world. She works in London, Los Angeles, New York, and throughout the world, in film, TV, theatre, and pop videos. Her work as an acting coach includes auditions, readings, monologues, script breakdown, on-set coaching, and character development. Dee Cannon has run scene study workshops at the Actor's Centre in London and gives master classes in LA, New York, Stockholm, Berlin, Gothenberg, Tel Aviv, Jerusalem, and the Philippines.

Phone: +44 (0) 758 631 3390
Web: www.deecannon.com/

22. Mel Churcher

Mel Churcher worked mainly as an actor and broadcaster for her first twenty years in the business. Her work included leading roles at the National Theatre and New Shakespeare Co. and extensive film and television work including classic series such as *Upstairs Downstairs, Edward VII,* and *Duchess of Duke Street.* Mel is a leading acting and voice coach. She also coaches a wide range of professionals from budding newcomers to top film stars like Daniel Craig, Angelina Jolie, Keira Knightley and Jet Li; from presenters like Raymond Blanc and Goldie to singers like Tricky and Joss Stone; from top corporate executives and lawyers to rugby union referees.

Phone: +44 (0) 777 877 3019
Web: www.melchurcher.com

23. Lynn Edmonstone

Lynn has worked in the profession for over 15 years. She graduated with a BA in Acting from East 15 Acting School and she holds a City & Guilds Teaching Course for Actors. She uses a variety of techniques in her work which include improvisation, Laban, method acting, and the Alexander Technique.

Phone: +44 (0) 770 317 5257
Web: www.lynnedmonstone.com

General web resources for actors and performers

1. American Film Institute

AFI is America's promise to preserve the history of the motion picture, to honor the artists and their work, and to educate the next generation of storytellers. AFI provides leadership in film, television, and digital media and is dedicated to initiatives that engage the past, the present, and the future of the moving image arts.

2021 North Western Avenue
Los Angeles, CA 90027-1657
Phone: +1 (323) 856-7600
Web: www.afi.com

2. The Internet Movie Database (IMDb)

The Internet Movie Database is an online database of information related to films, television programs, and video games. This includes actors, production crew personnel, and fictional characters featured in these three visual entertainment media. It is one of the most popular online entertainment destinations, with over 100 million unique users each month and a solid and rapidly growing mobile presence. IMDb was launched on October 17, 1990, and in 1998 was acquired by Amazon.com. As of February 16, 2013, IMDb had 2,434,085 titles and 5,075,983 personalities in its database, as well as 41 million registered users.

410 Terry Avenue N
Seattle, WA 98109-5210
Web: www.imdb.com

3. Actors Journey USA

Actors Journey USA is a team of professionals that have a lifetime of experience guiding actors properly throughout their journey in the business. Through their program, seven days or thirty days in LA, you can expect to perform in showcases at the iconic Oakwood, located in the heart of film and television, meet and audit with the best acting coaches, find the best affordable places to live, seek a part time job, and learn your way around LA.

2905 Victoria Pl
Coconut Creek, FL 33066-1319
Phone: +1 (954) 917-0474
Web: http://actorsjourneyusa.com

4. Casting Society of America

The premier organization for casting directors in film, television, theatre, and new media, the Casting Society of America seeks to uphold and honor the highest standards of professionalism in the casting field, to advocate and promote the role of the casting director generally and within the entertainment industry while supporting its members to further their goals and protect their common interests.

606 N. Larchmont Blvd., Suite 4-B
Los Angeles, CA 90004-1309
Phone: +1 (323) 463-1925
Web: www.castingsociety.com

5. Actors Casting & Talent Services

Actor Castings: Free casting calls in every state. Easy to view castings for TV shows, movies, feature films, game shows, reality shows, short films, and theatre. Auditions are being held daily.

30 NE 52nd Street
Oklahoma City, OK 73105
Phone: +1 (405) 702-0400
Web: www.actorscasting.com

6. Backstage

A Los Angeles edition, Backstage West, was launched in 1994, and Backstage.com came to life in 1997. Today, the Backstage brand signifies something greater than simply casting notices: Backstage is a place where actors, singers, and dancers can connect with the greater performing arts community. More importantly, Backstage is where performers can get all the information they need to succeed in the entertainment business. Actors browse through our weekly newspaper, checking updated production listings or reading our periodic spotlights on photography, college programs, acting schools, and coaches.

5700 Wilshire Boulevard, Suite 500
Los Angeles, CA 90036
Phone: +1 (323) 525-2356
Web: www.backstage.com

7. NYCastings

NYCastings is a fantastic website where talent can submit to film, TV, theatre, commercials, and print jobs. NYCastings has been a staple in the New York production community for the last 12 years, helping cast talent for hundreds of productions a month.

243 w. 30th St., 3rd Fl. (between 7th & 8th Aves.)
New York, NY 10001
Phone: +1 (212) 219-3339
Web: www.nycastings.com

8. Artists Health Insurance Resource Center

Artists Health Insurance Resource Center (AHIRC) has been connecting artists, craftspeople, and entertainment industry workers around the country to health insurance and affordable health care since 1998.

729 Seventh Avenue, 10th Floor
New York, NY 10019
Phone: +1 (212) 221-7300
Web: http://www.ahirc.org

9. ExploreTalent.com

Since its debut in 2003, ExploreTalent.com has become the Internet's largest audition, job, and casting call resource for actors, models, musicians, dancers, and production crew. It matches a talent's attributes against tens of thousands of audition and job postings every day. Explore Talent's unique technology sends casting email alerts and posts auditions and jobs directly on talents' profiles, saving members hours of time from tedious searching. Explore Talent has proven to be the best possible destination for talents with well over 7.5 million members and over 60,000 auditions, castings, and production jobs listed—40 times more postings than any other site!

3395 S Jones Blvd., Suite 15
Las Vegas, NV 89146
Phone: +1 (800) 598-7500
Web: www.exploretalent.com

10. Actingbiz.com

Actingbiz.com was created by actors, for actors. It provide free resources and guidance to be successful in all acting endeavors. Actingbiz provides free acting tips, acting advice, and guidance for actors and actresses of all ages.

Web: www.actingbiz.com

11. TheActingBiz.com

TheActingBiz.com is a social network for actors, dedicated to connecting casting directors, agents, actors, producers, crew, talent, industry players, and investors to get the project made starring actors.

Web: www.theactingbiz.com

12. Breakdown Services, Ltd.

Breakdown Services, Ltd. is the communications network and casting system that provides the most professional means to reach talent agents as well as actors when casting a project. In 1971 Breakdown Services started by delivering casting information to talent agents overnight via messenger. Today's Breakdown Service delivers casting information instantly via the Internet. Breakdown Services has offices in Los Angeles, New York, and Vancouver and maintains affiliate relationships with sister companies in Toronto, London, and Sydney. With clients in most regions of the USA and provinces of Canada, our reach extends throughout North America.

2140 Cotner Ave.
Los Angeles, CA 90025
Phone: +1 (310) 276-9166
Web: www.breakdownexpress.com

13. Actingland, Inc.

Actingland is the leading online casting solution for actors, actresses, and movie extras. Whether you are a beginner or a seasoned professional actor, Actingland has the practical information and instructions to help you find a talent agent, locate your next job, and nail your casting audition. Using any Internet-enabled device, talent agents, talent scouts, casting directors, managers, producers, and members of the filmmaking community can easily access Actingland's massive talent database, browse through the tens of thousands of actor portfolios, and perform in-depth searches for actors and actresses with the right characteristics and skills for their productions.

11271 Ventura Blvd. # 395
Studio City, CA 91604
Phone: none
Web: www.actingland.com

14. Casting Networks, Inc.

Casting Networks, Inc. is a software company dedicated to providing business solutions for entertainment professionals. By creating tools for communication, scheduling, media management, marketing, career development, and talent scouting, they are streamlining some of the most complex processes facing the industry and creating an environment that will make it easier for these professionals to find work and get their jobs done.

307 7th Avenue Suite 1507
New York, NY 10001
Phone: +1 (323) 462-8131
Web: http://home.castingnetworks.com/

15. StrawHat

StrawHat is an organization that supports the careers of non-equity actors and technical artists looking to start and continue their professional careers in the theatre. Its main activity is to produce the StrawHat Auditions, which are held in New York every spring. Over three days, more than 750 actors and "techies" and staff from over forty theatres attend. Actors audition for available positions in the theatre's summer seasons while technical people post their résumés and portfolios online and arrange phone or onsite interviews.

StrawHat Auditions 315
1771 Post Road East
Westport, CT 06880
Phone: +1 (203) 254-8572
Web: www.strawhat-auditions.com

16. BAFTA

The British Academy of Film and Television Arts (BAFTA) supports, promotes, and develops the art forms of the moving image—film, television and video games—by identifying and rewarding excellence, inspiring practitioners and benefiting the public. As the leading charity in the UK supporting the art forms of the moving image, BAFTA ensures that the very best creative work can be accessed and appreciated by the public.

195 Piccadilly,
London W1J 9LN
Phone: +44 (0)20 7734 0022
Web: www.bafta.org

17. Mandy.com

In 1995 Mandy.com was the first database of film/TV technicians and facilities on the web, today getting more than 5 million impressions per month. Mandy.com is listed in the first page in a Google search for film and TV production. Mandy.com offers six channels for TV/film production professionals: Services (yellow pages of technicians and facilities), LiveDiary (where employers can search for film/TV freelance crew by local town and date-availability), Casting (Casting calls searchable by gender, age and ethnicity), Jobs (For current job vacancies in film/TV production in your area), Classified (Buy/Sell production equipment), Film Market (Database of Films and TV Programs for sale. It assists independent producers to find niche sales in our fragmented marketplace).

Lighthouse Internet Ltd
Oasis Business Centre
85-87 Bayham Street
London NW1 0AG, England
Phone: +44 (0)20 7424 7817
Web: www.mandy.com

18. Listal

Listal is a social network based around entertainment including movies, TV shows, games, DVDs, m Msic and books, AActors & and actresses, Music artists, Authors, and Directors.

Suite 17677, Lower Ground Floor
145-157 St John Street
London EC1V 4PW
Phone: none
Web: www.listal.com

19. Actors' Benevolent Fund

The role of the Actors' Benevolent Fund is to care for actors and theatrical stage managers unable to work because of poor health, an accident, or frail old age. Generous support from members of the public and the acting profession itself means the Actors' Benevolent Fund has fulfilled this commitment to actors for over 125 years.

6 Adam Street
London WC2N 6AD
Phone: +44 (0)20 7836 6378
Web: www.actorsbenevolentfund.co.uk

20. The Actor's Café

The Actor's Café started in 2012 with two simple aims: 1) to provide mentoring support to young actors starting out in their careers, actors returning to work after a break, or for people deciding on a late career change. 2) to teach actor-friendly business techniques, helping other actors to change their mindset and provide resources and support, taking the hard work out of running a business and allowing the actor to be creative.

Phone: +44 (0)79 5892 1172
Web: www.theactorscafe.co.uk

21. CastNet

CastNet was formed in 1997 to provide a free service to the film, theatre and television industry seeking experienced, professional actors. CastNet has assisted over 10,000 casting directors and production companies in their requirements for talented and experienced actors for every kind of production.

20 Sparrows Herne, Bushey
Herts WD23 1FU

Phone: +44 (0)20 8420 4209
Web: www.castingnetwork.co.uk

INDEX

Symbols

50 Cent 55
54 Berners Street 51

A

agent 8, 16, 22, 29, 32, 57,
   59, 60, 65, 101, 103,
   104, 105, 107, 110,
   117
Anderson, Ron 28
Astaire, Fred 46
ATA/NATR 104
Atkinson, Rowan 18

B

Berry, Hale 28
Big Four 103

C

Cage, Nicolas 46
Carrey, Jim 14
celebrity 8, 9, 11, 13, 14,
   27, 37, 38, 43, 51
celebrity status 12, 30
Clooney, George 13, 14
Creative Artists 103
Cyrus, Miley 48

D

dialects 24
domain names 49

F

failure 117
Forbes 12

G

Garbo, Greta 46
gatekeeper 84, 92, 94, 96
goal 21, 24, 26, 33, 34, 37,
   63, 67, 69, 117
Gottfried, Gilbert 55
Grant, Cary 45

H

Haber, Margie 28
Hook, Theodore Edward
   51

I

International Creative
   Management 103
Izzard, Eddy 25

L

Lincoln, Abraham 31
London, Roy 22

M

mantra 116
media 9, 11, 38, 40, 54, 57
Michele, Lea 46
Montaigne 117
Moore, Demi 43
motivation 27, 32, 34, 118

N

name 11, 29, 40, 41, 42, 43, 44, 45, 46, 47, 48, 49

O

obstacle 67, 80, 81, 82

P

paparazzi 10
Perry, Luke 46
persistence 31, 34, 106
personality 14, 17, 29, 44, 73, 77, 78, 98, 107
Pitt, Brad 22, 28, 29, 43, 47
Portman, Natalie 47

R

Reid, Tara 38
résumé 29, 31, 33, 34, 106, 108
Roberts, Julia 43

S

SAG 33, 34, 41, 43, 104, 105, 110, 111, 112, 113, 115
SAG voucher 111, 112
sales 24, 63, 66, 71, 73, 80, 86, 88, 95, 98, 106, 109
Sheen, Charlie 47
show reel 107
Spears, Britney 48
stage names 41
status 10, 12, 28, 32, 37, 51

T

Thatcher, Margaret 118
The Wayback Machine 29
The William Morris Endeavor Agency 103
trademark 40, 47, 48, 49

U

United Talent Agency 103
urbanization 7

W

Wayne, John 45
website 27, 29, 49, 54, 108
Woods, Tiger 21

X

X-factor 13, 16

Y

Youtube 56